WALLS

WALLS

Poets Speak (while we still can), vol. 4

Edited by John Roche

Beatlick Press
&
Jules' Poetry Playhouse Publications
Albuquerque, NM

Poets Speak (while we still can) is a series of mini-anthologies addressing the current national and planetary crisis.

Series Editor: John Roche
Associate Editor: Jules Nyquist
Art Editor: Denise Weaver Ross

Cover Design: Denise Weaver Ross
Section I Illustration: Jules Nyquist, *Trinity Site Fence*
Section II Illustration: Margaret Randall, *Border Wall Near Sasabe*
Section III Illustration: Jules Nyquist, *Jornada del Muerto*
Section IV Illustration: Kevin Zepper, *Chaco*
Section IV Illustration: John Roche, *City of Rocks*
P. 38 Illustration: Janet Ruth, *Pomes*

Special thanks to Beatlick Press publisher Pamela Hirst
and Beatlick Press editor Deborah Woodside Coy!

ISBN-13: 978-1985244603
ISBN-10: 1985244608
Printed in the United States of America

All copyrights remain with the authors, artists and photographers

Cpyright ©2018 Beatlick Press and Jules' Poetry Playhouse Publications, all rights reserved.

Acknowledgments

The following poems have appeared elsewhere:

Megan Baldrige's "Pulling the Wool Over Our Eyes" appeared in *UNpresidented*, Jules's Poetry Playhouse Publications, 2017.

Rich Boucher's "McDonald's Hiring Poster" was first published at *In Between Hangovers* in Jan. 2017.

Michael Czarnecki's "Fenced in by History" is a section from his poem "Liberty Street Poetry Reading, Bath, NY" which has appeared in numerous places, beginning with *The Corning Leader* in 1988.

Katherine DiBella Seluja's "If You Need a Wall" was first published in *Sin Fronteras* (2010) and is also included in her forthcoming U New Mexico Press book, *Gather the Night*.

Douglas Lipton's "Birling Carrs" has appeared on the *New Boots and Pantisocracies* blog.

Ellaraine Lockie's "Waiting for Midnight" was first published in *Ruminate Magazine*, 2010.

John Macker's "On the Borderline with Pancho Villa" appeared in the *Santa Fe Literary Review* vol. 11, August 2016.

Maril Nowak's "Light and Dark: A Synthesis" won first prize and was published in *Visions & Viewpoints: Voices of the Genesee Valley*, 1994.

Jules Nyquist's "Imaginary Borders" was originally published in *Behind the Volcanoes*, Beatlick Press, 2014.

An earlier version of Colleen Powderly's "Jo Almost Despairs" appeared in *Mo' Joe: The Anthology*, Beatlick Press, 2014.

Preface

Walls is volume four of *Poets Speak (while we still can)*, a series of anthologies in response to the national and planetary crisis provoked by the election of 11/8/16. The other published volumes are titled *Trumped, Hers, and Water. Survival* is forthcoming.

All profits arising from this series will be donated to the following organizations: The American Civil Liberties Union, Southwest Women's Law Center, Indigenous Environmental Network, National Immigration Law Center, and Southern Poverty Law Center.

We wish to thank all the poets and artists who are contributing to this project!

Contents

1. Jules Nyquist, *Trinity Site Fence*
2. Michael Czarnecki, *Fenced in by History*
3. Hakim Bellamy, *Finish Line*
4. Marc Schillace, *Something There Is That Loves a Wall*
5. Steve Coffman, *A Wall Doesn't Have to Rhyme with Tall*
6. Martha Treichler, *Borders Do Not Have to Be*
7. Steve Ausherman, *Stacking Stones*
8. Eugene Stelzig, *Mr. Jones Revidius*
9. Mary McGinnis, *Snags*
10. Ellaraine Lockie, *Waiting for Midnight*
11. Ceinwen E. Cariad Haydon, *In or Out?*
12. Bill Nevins, *Shady Lady, Bright Tiger and the Builder of the Wall*
13. R.B. Warren, *In the Beginning*
15. Kitty Jospé, *Colors*
17. Randy Prus, *Of Monuments & Memorials*
18. Craig Czury, *The Wall*
19. Shelly Bryant, *Gentry*
20. Kathamann, *The Obstacle Race*
21. Katherine DiBella Seluja, *If You Need a Wall*

II.
24. Neil Young, *The Newer Colossus*
25. Joanne S. Bodin, *Where Chimera Fades*
26. Deborah Coy, *Channeling a Trump Supporter*
27. Vincent F. A. Golphin, *Recollection*
28. Gayle Lauradunn, *Too early yet for cherry blossoms*
30. Teresa Gallion, *Contagious Disease*
31. William Pruitt, *We Care More Now*
33. John Roche, *Tear Down the Walls!*
34. Herb Kauderer, *Lacking a Microscope*
36. Roslye Ultan, *Boulder Revelations*
37. Faith Kaltenbach, *Pome Poem*
39. Rich Boucher, *McDonald's Hiring Poster*
42. Larry Goodell, *Life Begins Where It Never Ends*
43. Cullen C. Whisenhunt, *The Wall*
45. Megan Baldrige, *Pulling the Wall Over Our Eyes*
48. Kenneth Gurney, *Hashtag*
49. Joshua Gage, *Tupilak in Cantaloupe Southern Diplomacy*
50. Georgia Santa Maria, *I Found a Golfball on the Border*

III.

54. Eleanor Grogg Stewart, *Do You Have a Secret?*
55. Robbie Sugg, *Passage*
56. Jennifer Maloney, *Fort Worth, February 2017*
58. Gretchen Schulz, *refugee*
59. Steve Ausherman, *Lengthening Shadows*
60. Lori Nolasco Martinez, *The Children Who Were Stopped on the Banks of the Rio Bravo*
61. Celeste Helene Schantz, *A Database of Exhumed Objects to Identify Those Who Perished*
62. Sylvia Ramos Cruz, *Give Me Your Tired*
64. Neil Young, *Window-seat on Eurostar*
66. Craig Czury, *The Border Crossing*
67. Douglas Lipton, *Birling Carrs*
68. Wayne Lee, *Migration*
69. Leah Zazulyer, *Bitter at Her*
71. Karin Bradberry, *Pantoum for Ra'ad Lalqaraghuli*
72. Lyn Lifshin, *Life in Aleppo*
73. Lyn Lifshin, *When the Borders Close*
74. Lori Nolasco Martinez, *Millennial Census-Taker*
75. John Macker, *Navigating the Archipelago of Treacheries*
76. Lawrence Welsh, *Rio Grande Roadrunner*
77. John Macker, *On the Borderline with Pancho Villa*
78. John Roche, *The Backpack*
79. Tina Carlson, *Deportations*
81. Scott Wiggerman, *Some of Them Were Dreamers*
82. Bart White, *My Brother's Keeper*
84. Mary Strong Jackson, *Dear Mexican Friend*
85. Jules Nyquist, *Imaginary Borders*
86. Stuart A. Paterson, *News*

IV.

88. Pamela Williams, *Destructive Construction*
89. Colleen Powderly, *Jo Almost Despairs*
90. Patricia Roth Schwartz, *Hat Poem*
91. M. J. Iuppa, *Next Time*
92. Maril Nowak, *Light & Dark: A Synthesis*
93. Nathanael William Stolte, *All the Screens Between Us*
94. Steven Deridder, *Don't Ever Forget*
95. Karin Bradberry, *Standing for Your Name*
96. Leah Zazulyer, *Café, Cincinnati Airport*
97. Loren Niemi, *Not the Date*
98. Mina Hatami, *Closed Doors*
100. Janet Ruth, *Cage*

102. Jane Lipman, *Extraterrestrial*
103. Linda Yen, *Therapy at the Healthplex*
105. Margaret Baumler, *Where Do Dreams Go?*

V.
108. Margaret Randall, *Louder*
109. G. E. Schwartz, *If There Is a Wall*
110. Dennis Maloney, *from Border Crossings #4*
111. Dennis Maloney, *from Border Crossings #5*
112. Loren Niemi, *Kabir on the Border*
113. Don Paul, *Goodbye, Walls*
114. Stewart S. Warren, *When You Come Upon a Prisoner*
115. Dwain Wilder, *The Tiny House*
116. Mary Elizabeth Lang, *Deconstructing "Mending Wall"*
118. Mary Dudley, *On the Birth of the Nigerian Twins*
119. Eleanor Grogg Stewart, *The Walls of Time*
120. Randy Prus, *On Turner & Time, too*
121. Bruce Noll, *A Time to Bring Stones Together*
122. Bruce Noll, *Builders*
123. Renny Golden, *Magicians*
124. Bill Nevins, *Wind Fall*
126. Karla Linn Merrifield, *Wherehow*
128. Mary Strong Jackson, *On Both Sides of the Wall*
129. Janet Eigner, *On the Way Down*
130. Janet Eigner, *Higher Math*
131. Dick Bakken, *Without Walls*
133. Annette Velasquez, *No Borders*
134. Janet Ruth, *As If They Were Not There*
136. Kate Marco, *leap*
137. Andrew Prokop, *Clearly Certainly Yes*

Addenda:
139. Bios
151. Publishers' Page

Another World Is Possible!
¡Si, Se Puede

I.

Jules Nyquist, *Trinity Site Fence*

Michael Czarnecki

Fenced in by History

Like animals behind electric fencing,
shocked once or twice
while trying to reach out
over the line,
we keep well within boundaries.
What's learned the hard way, sticks.
No need to catch that jolt again.

But have you checked lately?
Maybe the charger's run dead.

Hakim Bellamy

Finish Line

The skin wears no borders
born devoid the separation
of garment and genitalia.

Only lines of wrinkle
and palm, other than
the occasional ebb and wane
of varicose.

Where the skin turns in on itself
like a fold,
rather than apart
like a zipper.

There is no way out
of this body, this membrane
is all windows and walls.
No doors.

The hollow deck
just beyond the fleeting line of lids
post blink.

The shifting shoreline
of frown and smile that
curtain teeth from time
to time, like a mirage.

The skin lies continuous.
Uninterrupted by the migration
of hairlines.
Unconquered by the cracked earth
crawl of laugh lines 'cross the desert
of our temples.

Only separable
in our once limitless
imaginations,
just like the face
of the Earth.

Marc Schillace

Something There Is That Loves a Wall

I was born from the walls of my mother's uterus
dropped into hospital walls
fed from milk bottles on the front wall of my mother
I banged my head on many walls
I had balls for breaking down walls

There are walls everywhere in the world
Physical, social and economic walls
Walls based on education
Walls around knowledge crammed into little fiefdoms
And walls of ignorance in large vats

Walls are boundaries
Bodies are boundaries between where I end and others begin
The relative world is ever changing boundaries
Walls that define place, space, parks and prisons
There are walls around nuclear missiles and daycare centers
There is Wall Street
Something there is that loves a wall

Every house has walls
A home is the heart space between walls
The loving heart has no walls
The loving heart knows no boundaries
The loving heart transcends boundaries
Dissolves the barriers of differences and experience
The loving heart is receptive to the other
Embraces common humanity as the barriers fall
Something there is that still loves a wall

Steve Coffman

A Wall Doesn't Have to Rhyme with Tall

Walls are something like teeth, or a lovely barrier reef
that keeps out dirt and surf, quiets the tongue.

Some walls are to keep dogs in, while giving them the illusion
that they're free.

Other walls are simply failures of neighborly discourse:
Concrete expressions of ego. Foregoing negotiation.
Forestalling common ground.

Walls make dandy markers for remembering our wisest heads
or prematurely dead. Also handy for provoking conversation,

Inciting alarm at evil unseeable ones on wall's other side.
Cramping brain cells, fostering evermore blubbery words, rubbery legs
or lethal arms.

Unless, of course, one's high enough to oversee both sides. From outer
spaces, see how small even the Great Wall of China really is –
hardly much at all.

Martha Treichler

Borders Do Not Have to Be

Borders do not have to be
walls of stone,
do not need
watch towers with
soldiers and guns
to keep folks out.

A border can have bridges
that cross rivers,
can have gates that open
to let visitors in,
a sign to say, "Welcome!"

A border is not real,
is only a fantasy someone uses
to say, "This is mine!"
Negotiations then must start.

There is no right side
of the border,
no wrong side.
If we do not negotiate and compromise
we are no better than cousin orangutan
who bares his teeth with murderous intent
at those who cross his border.

Steve Ausherman

Stacking Stones

We can erect walls to keep out our fears, but we will fail.
We can stack stone upon stone, but our backs will be no stronger.

Mortar and stone, steel and slab, rebar and rust, wood and wire.
The components of construction are heavy in our hands.

Shovel and hammer, bulldozer and grater, pickaxe and trowel.
We build and resist. Persist and plunder. Burrow and plow.

Our walls keep out our enemies. Our walls keep out our friends.
Our walls constrain the rising sun. Our walls cordon off a silver moon.

The desert will swallow our walls. Can't we possess a long view?
We build a band of snaking metal and I am reminded of my own flaws.

These border walls will outlast my sagging skin and aging bones,
But I prefer an elegy of worn volumes resting upon a bookshelf.

We risk constructing museums where all we store are the rusted girders
That illuminate how small we once were. How bereft of solutions.

How will we look, peering out over the parapets of our barricades?
Strong or scared? Masterful or malevolent? Virtuous or vindictive?

We can erect walls to keep out our fears, but we will fail.
We can stack stone upon stone, but our backs will be no stronger.

Eugene Stelzig

Mr. Jones Revidius

You don't know Mr. Jones
do you that the walls
you build to keep others
out will lock you in
to feed your fears
and shrink the horizon
of who you might be
to the disappearing
shadow of your best self.

Give Urizen enough rope
and he will tie his own
hands and feet
to fret himself away
in endless grief.

Build your walls,
imprison yourself,
feed your fears,
drown in your tears,
won't you,
Mr. Jones,
your very flesh
shrunk off your bones.

Mary McGinnis

Snags

So I can walk over them,
now I walk backwards over them,
along with exploding them, I
give them to a god who
says "Shucks,

"in another life I wore a dress
I was much smaller then.

"I began to invent a poison country called division;
it made a lot of people keel over,
it made a lot of people leave home.

"Next time around, I vow 'small' will not rule;
small will not insist on electro-shock for the confused;
small will expand and become
an element everywhere.

"No longer tripping myself up,
alone, but not really—I
give my rainbow pockets a shake, and out come
serenity, silliness, an
invisible bag of bliss."

Ellaraine Lockie

Waiting for Midnight

My grandson says *Ouma, you're just like Cinderella*
as I feed carrots and kale to five rabbits in the backyard
Seeds to the squirrels and twenty-some species of birds
Walnuts and dry cat food for the crows
I believe he expects me to entice them all
into my art studio to design a gown for the evening

We don't talk anymore about the mouse my cat caught
when he learned life isn't always a fairy tale
He knows by now I don't believe in cages or walls
and that there should be only one zoo in every country
What he doesn't know is how insignificant
that glass slipper is

How searching for it can rust the years from their hinges
Open doors into rooms that breathe Marlboro
smoke, whiskey and musk oil
Ghost of the male deer donor hanging from a rafter
Men with oiled skin that lusters like a yellow canary diamond
who smell the scent of longing and hunt it down

Catch and release until they're bored with the wounds
and slam the door in your face
Yet you open another before scabs form
Until finally you're bled dry and forced to heal
You learn to meditate in your backyard
To watch a banana blossom unfold

I tell none of this to my grandson
He'll have to discover for himself
the difference between authentic and synthetic
How the latter is only snake oil
That a fence around a place isn't always a cage
but protection from the other side
And that even a castle has a wall or moat

Ceinwen E. Cariad Haydon

In or Out?

When we came, we put a wooden fence at the bottom of our garden. Annie, our new neighbour asked, 'To keep folk out or keep you in?' Strange to her, this choice of ours. Were we nude sunbathers? No, of course not. It's cold, in northern Britain.

When a bad lad and his girl set up home in our village, people watched, gossiped censoriously. Fences went up all over, edges spiked with glass for certainty. Really? Yes, sure, of course. It's wild, in northern Britain.

When food supplies thinned and water rations dribbled, we built a high wall to keep what's ours. A stone circle with one door, the door had one key, the key hung round the headman's neck. Safe now? Never, not nowadays. Danger lurks, in northern Britain.

When the plague came, the headman died first, no one cried, but all were terrified. Folk screamed for cures to halt the pestilence. A brave girl said she'd go outside the walls to find herbs and healers. She could not exit. We'd lost the key, in northern Britain.

Bill Nevins

Shady Lady, Bright Tiger and the Builder of the Wall ("In the forests of the night")

Two doors stood before them:
the shaded door
and the bright white sunlit one.
The lost white families feared the shade
and the beckoning Lady
who lives there
so they chose the other door
and fled to the safe- hold fortress
to which they were invited
by the great white builder
as a white tiger prowls among them purring.
They don't worry
for the tiger is a good pet
the wall builder has said.
It catches mice and such.
When the tiger begins to devour them
slowly one by one at first
then by dozens
still purring,
the doors, they find,
are locked
and they see the walls around them--
once so very white,
now running with their rusting blood.
Then the great wall builder pets his purring tiger
as he collects their gnawed white bones
to build his walls
and he smiles.
Now, the white families huddle
in the white-lit rooms
of the white fortress
celebrating their safety,
trying to dance in their
stiff white bodies
trying so hard
to dance

R.B. Warren

In the Beginning

Darkness covered the void.
And there was no light.
In the beginning of a new beginning,
Light covered the void and darkness
And wherever the light was, the darkness could not be.
And in all the countless, myriad,
Beyond measure, beginnings and endings
From the first, even unto this day,
Light and darkness have contested to begin
And renew each restive beguiling creation.

The first killer killed first in the light,
And fled to the safety of shadowland caves.
Sheltered and holiest marked for the flight,
He played with the unseen, touch-only toys,
Until the cave absorbed the lightness of touch
And the breathing, breath-taking of bloodiest joys.

Light fluttered into the darkness
Where the sounds, the unseen noises,
Became the voices of fear and trembling,
Of a world reduced, compacted, boiled down,
To the leftover stickiness of blood and the blind
Untouchable threat that could not see
The forehead mark of safety.

His life now required the light.
And he speaks a second time, and asks,
Am I my god damned brother's keeper?
Or my keeper's god damned brother?
Are you and I one in the same?
Am I to love the manacles, the chains,
Joined at the hip with the one
Who watches the bars
And creates the echoed hallways?
The razor wire and the locks?
Am I to love this self-made enemy?
This one who seeks to kill me
With the safety of his mark.
This one who has marked me,

My family, my kin as death?
This one through me has introduced
Death into the world and marked me free
And safe from all injury.
Am I to love the kill
And worship the lying sacrifice
That much?

Who appointed these walls of separation?
The foundations to be created, the doorposts
Resting on the bodies of your precious ones.
What will you fashion now from your blood-soaked dirt?
Is it my self-love, or yours, that will create
More than has been consecrated?
Who will create death and pain and suffering?
Again and again and again.
If not you?
Can you bear to bear your guilt
Made safe by you in me?

We have covered each other, all of us,
With the blood sanctified in your way
Of continuing creation.
You have granted us the knowledge
Of the openings that seep or gush
The blood, cells, and plasma,
And fluids secretly demanded
To fulfill and foul your killing ground.

Later killers will create the first city,
Ramparts, enclosures, enclaves,
The walls, another creation of the us
And the not-us. The other, totally
The other. The first stand-in
For you, your hierarchy,
Your competition.

AAh! The first altar.
Not a tower at all. Only raised up
For the blood to drain down
And be seen by us
And the not-us over the wall,
And for all to be terrorized.
Your choreography is magnificent.

Kitty Jospé

Colors
              (with a nod to Dunya Mikhail)

The generals post a map,
draw boundaries a child could color:
purple for Iraq,
yellow, Syria
blue, Kuwait
red, Afghanistan
green, Vietnam.

The child will not draw black lines
that lead to missiles,
black crosses for intended battles.

No, the child draws wisteria,
so it swings in the wind over
a field of wild flowers:

sweet violets
delicate, but proliferous;

buttercups, for children to pick and put under the chin,
laughing, to ask, *Do you like butter?*,
before they know about luxury or humility;

forget-me-nots whose small faces fill with fidelity to loved ones,
despite separation or other challenges
before they know about Alzheimer's or the Armenian genocide;

poppies for remembrance
before they know about Flanders
and the First World War;

the lush greens of the Bells of Ireland,
said to represent luck
before they know about Hallmark cards
and appropriated holidays.

The child does not know the colors
display the effects of American engagement:
For Iraq, purple-stained fingers;

For Syria, yellow mushroom of the chemical attack;
For Kuwait, blue passport, failed revolution;
For Afghanistan, Red Cross, Red Crescent, and those poppies, opiates;
For Vietnam, green leaf kratom, to relieve pain, aid for withdrawal.

The child perhaps once thought colors fall from rainbows,
like promises in the story of Noah's Ark—
what lies in the map of wars:
smart, beautiful colors
waving standards
for killing.

It ends for us all in the color of dust.

Randy Prus

Of Monuments & Memorials

> *Monuments commemorate the memorable and embody the myths of beginnings. Memorials ritualize remembrance and mark the reality of ends.* —Arthur Danto, "The Vietnam Veterans Memorial." *The Nation.* 31 Aug. 1985.

...what we do is
what we do, the dog's
business barks morning...

...he doesn't have last
night's meal with coffee,
a cigarette, the NYTimes...
...he prefers the cooling
of summer, a walk in rain,
a sniff of those before him...

...he leaves a memorial,
a moment of the past...
...we cling to monuments,
a present directing a future...
a statue to our own being..
...his grammar differs from ours...
but not by much....today,
I took a monumental shit,
and flushed it away....

Craig Czury

The Wall

The assignment is to draw a picture of your family. Here's my house. Here's my mom. Here's my dad. Here's my... The art teacher tells me to try to flesh out my stick figures, and hands me a stub of chalk. This is really a good idea. I trace the outline of my stick house...it becomes a huge wall. My teacher says good, now position everyone inside this open space to fill the borders. I stand my sister up against the wall and chalk her outline. Really good, Craig, now pose her, and the others, into what they do best, then chalk them in. Here's the chalk outline of my sister tangled around some strange boy in the back of his car...looks like she's at Knoebels on the roller coaster. Here's the outline of my mom spazzing out on the floor with a seizure...looks like she's at the stove stirring a brothy cacciatore. Here's my chalkline dad chasing me through the house with a leather strap...looks like he's fly fishing. The chalk outline of me sneaking out of my bedroom window at night is me climbing the wall.

Shelly Bryant

Gentry

around each garden, a wall
not great, imposing or impregnable
but capable of holding secret joys within
protecting the privacy of homely concerns

not great, imposing or impregnable
the unadorned whitewashed facades
protecting the privacy of homely concerns
stand straight and silent and well-mannered

the unadorned, whitewashed facades
hiding the women and men who
stand straight and silent and well-mannered
in the cultivated confines of refinement

hiding, the women and men who
are adept in guarding their secrets
in the cultivated confines of refinement
make of each garden, a wall

Kathamann

The Obstacle Race

from here to there
what do I take/bring

is one side warmer/colder
is the air cleaner

over there

beyond the barricades

I hate razor wire.

What language is spoken/written
Others occupy both sides of a wall.

Katherine DiBella Seluja

If You Need a Wall

Gather moon grey
fieldstones black

river rock beetles,
level your ground

extract every weed.
Divining rod in hand

consider its height.

Let the children etch
curlicue y's and g's.

Your neighbor will lean
there careless

robin might drop a twig.
Wild lily and gourd will curl

at its base   mix mortar
water from your father's well

or your grandmother's almanac.
Summer may wrap it in heat

ice will brittle each crevice.
There's room for crayon drawings,

his wide-ruled love note,
Saint Anne's birthday card.

It will contain your life,
leave it open

for chocolate brown quail,
mud to frost each layer
or blue pebbles picked from the shore.

You'll need a stout trowel
work swiftly,
mortar sets faster than grief.

II.

Margaret Randall, *Border Wall Near Sasabe*

Neil Young

The Newer Colossus

(With apologies to Emma Lazarus)

Liberty's been recast, and where she stood
So steadfastly between the great harbours
A dark form looms. Look for her familiar
Beacon in vain: snuffed out. Bullwhip and hood
Now drape the plinth, a Guantanamo rod
Glows fist-high to warn all within radar:
Turn your boats back, turn 'em back, hey stranger,
Fuck your sob-story and fuck your false God.
As for your 'poor and your huddled masses',
'Wretched refuse' (they're human trash, for sure):
Get real, amigo, we're kicking asses,
It's time for walls, not more damned golden doors
For every Mick, Spick, Abdullah or Juan.
Why? Don't shit me. Just know we can; I can.

Joanne S. Bodin

Where Chimera Fades

Skewed walls of illusion hold us hostage while
Global warming denial crashes along flood-damaged shorelines.
Immigrants flee in masses from tyrannical dictators.
The class divide indemnifies the status quo.
The sanctity of religious institutions justifies ethnocentrism.
Smells of liturgical incense mask betrayal and lust.
Rage goes awry when people cannot cry after being beaten down.
Lines at food banks snake around city streets.
The displaced, misplaced, replaced can't jolt us out of indifference
Even in the humbled face of reality.

Deborah Coy

Channeling a Trump Supporter

I was satisfied with a line on a map
until you trumpeted crisis
now I want a wall.
Make it immensely high
because I've seen how "those people"
can climb. Bury it deeper than
hell, because I understand "they" dig tunnels.
I know every Mexican
is a "bad hombre"
"They" will take my job!
Screw the cost.
Screw the habitats.
Forget abuela, tío and prima.
Make Mexico pay!
Make US safe again.

I was satisfied with truth
until you called it fake news,
now I want alternative facts.
Words I can shout,
Facts that fit my hate,
facts I can use
like fingers in my ears.
Facts spoken to mirrors.
Facts I can repeat,
a litany of hearsay to battle
this black brown yellow
rainbow miasma.

I was satisfied with my country
until you pointed out
how very very bad it was.

Vincent F. A. Golphin

Recollection

Remember who you were before 9/11,
before you stared twice into every brown, tan, and black face,
when anyone seated next to you
was a person, not an "ally," or "terrorist,"
how you once thought more about love than fear.

A voice among millions throughout the Earth,
recall the old century when
many people hoped for better, and believed
a chance to reach higher or farther
was within your grasp.

Americans did not spy on neighbors,
that happened in "bad countries" in Hollywood films,
or "somewhere in Russia," as they used to say.
you did not investigate those who might be friends,
nor profile those with different accents.

You never worried about the dangers that come from speaking out,
Nor that a plea for dialogue could cause you to face threats,
or that this country might be hated by some unnamed "other,"
from places, visible only in a president's imagination,
nor shrink in terror at sounds in the darkness.

Gayle Lauradunn

Too early yet for cherry blossoms

those thirteen varieties
like thirteen colonies
perfuming the Capitol
every spring
the lush array—
white
light pink
yellow
dark pink
even green
that dreaded color
of paradise
But we imagine
the fragrances to come
and how like the colors
they reflect what some
would wall over
It all may wither before
its time in the blast
of retrograde air emanating
from a soiled white edifice
A new awareness
we steal from
fast growing rubble
where cherry blossoms ebb

And like the blossoms
we are a sea of shapes:
triangular
columnar
v-shape
flat-topped
weeping

It's hard to imagine
but we can dream: he raises
both hands palms out
as though patting the air
his words heated
as though becalming us

as though he is not
fomenting conflict
as though he speaks
with honey not vinegar

The moon glows and, perhaps,
the sun will rise
Pink and white and green
blossoming

Teresa Gallion

Contagious Disease

The species Homo Sapiens has always
built physical and emotional barriers,
passed from one generation to the next.

Many groups fled other Countries to avoid
persecution, hunger and rejection.
They came to the Americas, staked claims
on nature and built fences to block others.

Every group fought against blockades
and carved a space they called their own.
Once settled, they created rejection walls
for the next group of settlers.

We find ourselves in the 21st century
and every group that fought and foraged space
now rejects those who want to come
into this space called America.

It seems to be a contagious disease
constructing walls against immigrants.
Mankind has not worked to find a cure.

William Pruitt

We Care More Now

> *Get 'em outta here!*—Donald Trump, during speech

Once there was a country made itself into
a giant pyramid scheme, it worked
for a while as long as the ones at the bottom
kept believing, but as people forgot
how to think, the promises in the chain letter
became incoherent and the ones not far from the bottom
started to panic and demand their share and in their fear
they lost empathy, their only real treasure
and connection to the great world
    Get 'em outta here!

So no more making nice in civil discourse
the rich who made the poor more poor
started helping them to hate the poorer yet
(though some realized a Chernobyl of collective hate
with no OFF switch might be a mistake)
but the refrain began and would not stop
Someone was responsible for no flavor in the bread,
no joy in Sunday hymn
    Get 'em outta here!

They never mattered except to build the country
now they complain, now they want more
it's not enough we let them in
it's not enough we gave them freedom
they think they're special
they don't understand American Exceptionalism,
they'd find out if they were in North Korea:
    Get 'em outta here!

The ones at the top have a game that the ones below
don't know about. Let's play grow up in a ghetto.
Let's play tie your hands behind your back now shake my hand.
Let's play the shadow game. We'll pretend you are equal to me.
You can use my water fountain. We'll even
swim in the pool together! But can you see
the shadow of your skin in my smile?
    You missed it game over!

Get 'em outta here!

Some say this hate is
what we've come to.
but think about it

slaves have been around
since before the pyramids
we were just too busy being afraid
to care too much about that
too busy being needy
around that strong man
with the whip

but it just so happens
enough of us can still think
who care more now
than we could or did
at the scary pyramids.

We care more now about the ones
from the next neighborhood
they are not equal to us because
they are not numbers and neither
are we. They are human beings
and we care more now than we used to.

John Roche

Tear Down the Wall!

When will we stop allowing barracudas and speculators to define
        prosperity?
Adopt a sane index to take our measure
Based on how well we treat each other and the planet
Not limited by borders of any kind.

Points for how many clothed, fed, housed, educated in the past month?
Points for how much conserved, how green is my city?
Points for climate not changed, globe not warmed,
        production not increased
Points for paying everyone more for fewer hours worked.

A stocking exchange where the object is to lose, generosity the gain
A place for individuals and nations to contribute money and work hours
Pick up the slack, help anyone in need
Prestige points for giving it away, not trumping others in the
        gimme game.

Herb Kauderer

Lacking a Microscope

> "Every man takes the limits
> of his own field of vision
> for the limits of the world."
> —*Schopenhauer*

Those obsessed with hugeness cannot see
beneath the borders of their grandiosity
to three hundred million pebbles
supporting an ego that reaches so far up
it loses touch with the earth beneath.

The mental screen for visualization rests
up and left, a location troubling
in its distance from cleavage
leading to a leader whose head tilts down
and can no longer find its left.
Down and right is the attitude
for imagining sensory imagery
such as newscasts of alternative facts
or criminal charges for those
on the enemies list.

The macroeconomy blinds him
to the microeconomy, to even the concept
of want and dearth and unfair advantages
and 60-hour work weeks devoid
of martinis and servants
as his star-studded cast of advisors
all stand within his huge field of vision
sparkling with their privilege

and even his populist weakness,
text versions of the tiny tweets
of many small and distant birds,
cannot penetrate his grandiosity.

Beneath his cosmic field of vision
a country whose DNA demands
individual opportunity
gathers steam, fogging grandiose eyes

that see in the resulting vagueness
grand schemes, rather than discharges
from a double boiler
placed exactly beneath his chair.

Roslye Ultan

Boulder Revelation

Interpretation
Dashes of color at the top of a hill on four acres of open field emanate from a radiant quartet of forty tons of massive rocks partially masked by blue, pink, lavender and gold shiny steel sheets volleying for sunlight by day, reflecting the moon and stars at night, and each of us walking among them. Rain waters splash over them sending a stream of sparkling messages, and in winter snow wraps them in warm white sweaters. Each boulder contains four hundred million years of stories to be discovered. This field a gathering place for dance performances, film screenings, concerts, and summertime picnics is where teens steal kisses and children whimsically hide and seek between giant rocks adorned in fancy dress.

Construction
This *quartet of boulders* caused me to reflect on the tower-wall of rugged gray rocks stacked on a slope overlooking my backyard - once woodland for wild turkeys, red fox, warblers, cardinals, ducks, and geese now deprived of their natural habitat ravaged several yards from my house - a *stone's throw* from the waters of Minnehaha Creek. No longer does sunlight shine through the trees, or rain sparkle on leafs, nor can we see the setting sun blocked by a 30ft high wall because one person decided to root up the magic of wilderness to support construction for a private playground. No love for perfection of rock formations, or the singular necessity for trees, rather indifference for nature, and the very notion of existence and nourishment for planetary sustainability. *Oh, where, oh where* has all the reverence gone for the sun's warmth, the cool moon, and the radiant constellations eclipsed by a wall of stone.

Faith Kaltenbach

Pome Poem
                (after Li-Young Li "This Hour and What Is Dead")

Tonight an apple, over there in the fruit bowl,
is whispering to the others. I can just hear her
from my podium here on the buffet.
Why do apples always talk behind our backs?
Why doesn't she stay in her proper place,
making pies and keeping the doctor away?
Even here in amazing beautiful Banana Palace,
any pome can be a traitor. They're dangerous.

At this hour, anyone whispering is bad
and anyone listening is out of control.

Someone tell the stupid apple she belongs in the kitchen.

Tonight a pear lies smugly on his bed of paper towels.
They don't want his delicate skin to get bruised.
They're saving him for a weekend dinner party.
What is a pointy-head pear good for anyway?
Why do they rave about his exquisite taste?
All he does is drizzle down their chins.
He's just another example of the lightweight pomes,
the ones who threaten our terrific Banana Values.

At this hour anyone pear-shaped is trouble
and anything S-curved is crooked.

Someone tell the loser pear to learn to play golf.

Tonight a quince snores in the fruit bowl.
He's fuzzy, spotted, weak and lumpy.
They can't even wake him except by cooking him.
Why bother with such an idiot fruit?
Can't they smell him? It's all over the palace.
Our classy girls call him the ugliest boy in the bowl.
Yeah, he's typical of the three pomes,
a huge threat to united fruits and Banana Security.

At this hour anyone slow is useless
and the one who holds us back is a zero.

Someone tell the moron quince to just go away.

Unlike all the other fruits in the tremendous Banana Majority,
the weird flesh of the pomes grows from the stem.
Half stem, half flower! Disgusting! I don't want to think about it.

Note: Of the approximately 2000 kinds of edible fruits in the world only three (the apples, pears and quinces) are pomes. The flesh of pomes grows not from the flower but from the swollen stem end found just below the flower. Bananas are the most popular fruit in the world.

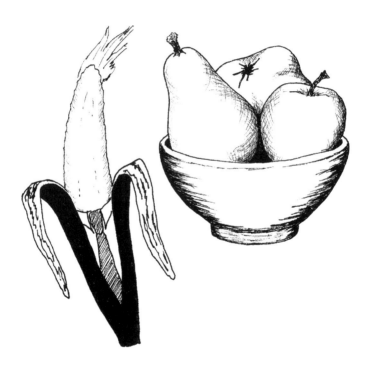

Janet Ruth

Rich Boucher

McDonald's Hiring Poster

In the first vision,
I see the McDonald's Hiring Poster
the way I first saw it in my life,
the way I first lived in 1986 in my life,
when I got that first job
just after high school and right before forever,
back in that manager's office
and there were nine of them,
nine free Americans all smiling at me
from just inside of that bright red and yellow poster.
Standing in tight 3 by 3 formation
and viewed from an angelic vantage point above them all,
they were every race and creed and sexual flavor,
all with the same exact *exact white teeth*,
African-Americans, white dudes and a winking pink dudette
and every shade of the rainbow
grinning together in name-tagged, two-dimensional harmony,
gay straight elderly heavy-set nerdy tough and milk-fed
these stepford paragons gazed upon me lovingly
knowing that I was about to join *the greasy slavery*,
all nine of them looking at me
and I swore I saw them all licking their lips
as I waded slowly in, waded
until I was up to my chest in a swamp of cooking oil
and everything was *America*
and I had to smile because I had a Coke
and America coated me in a sheen of submission;
I was her boy.

In the second vision,
inspired by the lifetime experience
of serving the public
which has always meant serving the Devil
which has always meant minimum wage for maximum abuse
I see it: the McDonald's Hiring Poster
frighteningly, fearsomely out of the frantic dark,
harshly spot-lit on a musty cellar wall
in the swinging, off-kilter glare of my unsteady flashlight
as I run and then stop, whirl around,
panting and terrified in a most lost and very haunted house;

all nine multiracial and multi-sexual and multi-trans
candidates for fast food employment
lift their bowed heads and then their happy faces *change*,
morph into scowls; I see the eyes on all nine
hollow out in an instant, their glares
floating quickly and irrevocably straight for me
from the depths of their empty eye sockets.

In the third vision,
I see the McDonald's hiring poster
tumbling up in the dark of the night air,
aloft on a stinking, apocalyptic breeze,
half-crumpled, one corner ablaze
like I just missed whoever lit it with a lighter
and I can see the multi-hued and multi-identity
McDonald's employees:
the young African-American girl
the older white lady
the middle-aged guy whose ethnicity I can't know
the teen person who I think is trans
like it matters what I either think or guess anymore
and they are all, together, unlike any hiring poster
I have ever seen; they're not looking at me at all:
they don't care if I want the job or not;
they don't care if I get hired or not;
instead they are bickering and fighting with each other,
shoving and screaming into each other's faces
like as if as though just like they were at an American rally
that was held in America to talk about America,
just like America has become one big angry rally
and melting pot screaming match;
I can make out the legend
welcome to the team
at the headline at the top of the poster
as the flames burn on, eating up the people
who once smiled at me
because McDonald's once McDonalded them
into whole, actualized contributors
to the economy.

In the fourth vision,
I see the McDonald's hiring poster
years and years and uncountable years
after the presidency of the Monster,

after America switched back to black and white,
after decades and decades of nuanced full-color,
after the end of the era of facts and truth;
I see the McDonald's hiring poster,
faded to a quiet, mere pastel of its former dayglo,
dilapidated, only three rusted staples fixing it
steady to a billboard outside in the rain,
the rain making every face on that hiring poster cry;
all nine prospective McDonald's team members weep,
wail and moan from the confines of the poster;
some of them reach to cover their mouths
to stop the sobbing
at the same time that I do;
why do these visions come to me now,
why do these visions come at all,
how many more will there be,
and what do they mean?

Who is the person
who can explain,
who can answer?

Larry Goodell

Life Begins Where It Never Ends

(put on black robe)

Speed ends desire as the turning over of the fire deepens —
crashing into the wall of beginning
who built the wall, there was
nobody here before us.
We are the major pigment in the painting of ourselves
the font of holy wisdom, the font of fonts
the fountain of fountains:
how dare these be a precedent before us?
We have already written the definitive text of our exact God.
Who dare question who we come from.
Just because we speed ahead & crash into a wall
doesn't mean the wall exists.
We won't have it. God won't have it.
Louie won't have it. Louie wrote the text of our one & only God.
Louie, Herbert, Bruce, & Joe.
They say no. Our God is **Hullabaloo**.
And it will always be **Hullabaloo**.
Those pigmy perverts who live on the other side of the wall
they worship Hooey. Hooey Youee Hooey! We say
We don't consider them at all. The infidels.
The lost. The damned. They're in the Hell they're going to.
But we'll get them to worship **Hullabaloo**, before we're through.
But the wall doesn't exist at all.
Nothing came before us, as Louie Herbert Bruce & Joe
have written down the word of **Hullabaloo**
when **Hullabaloo** said start, we started.
When he say don't pick your nose, don't defecate in public.
We don't do it. It is the line of wisdom straight back to his heart.
There is no wall before us, no other creatures, no other history
but what Louie Herbert Bruce & Joe have avowed
Written down from the mulling face of God, **Hullabaloo**.
Oh the wall is speaking. It can't! The wall we ran into does not exist.
                              (sing in 2 tones)
"We are bacteria. Back to bacteria. Back to back bacteria.
The wall of beginning. And ending bacteria."

Cullen C. Whisenhunt

The Wall

"Build the Wall!" you scream,
"Build the Wall!"

I say, who needs a wall when you have train tracks?
Those are hard enough to cross already,
And that's where all the "illegal" stuff goes, anyways,
To "the wrong side of the tracks."
People say it so nonchalantly,
Like "the wrong side of the bed."
As if they think you can go to sleep,
Roll over, and wake up on
The right side of the tracks.
Just like they think
They can go to sleep and wake up rich.
Sleepwalking their way to success
The new American Dream.

I wonder if immigrants ever think
About the American Dream,
Or if they only think about
The Land of Opportunity?
The difference, of course, being the distance between
The right and left rail.
The right side and the wrong side.

Don't build the Wall, I say,
Build Walls!

Build walls across the tracks, in the ghettos
    (not around, *in*).
Build walls to replace the ones that have fallen
    and caved in, and crumbled
Build walls for houses, and schools, and grocery
    stores, and hospitals.
Build walls for the homeless in their lean-tos
    and boxes,
And don't forget to put roofs on 'em,
    for the rain,
And windows and doors in 'em,

        so they know that walls can never fully separate
        us from each other.

Build walls around Wall Street,
        and bars and barbed wire, too.
Build the world's most well-stocked white-collar prison
        for all the men who imprison others with their bars of gold.
Build walls around every millionaire and billionaire
        in their ivory towers with wall to wall
        silver gilding.

Build Walls!
Walls!

But,
If you must build your Border Wall,
If you absolutely must,
Build it all the way around.
Don't stop at the Gulf.
Don't stop at Baja.
Build from California to Florida,
From Florida to Maine,
From Maine to Washington,
And from Washington back down to SoCal.
(Oh, and don't forget Alaska and Hawaii.)
Build it all the way around
And all the way up.
So high you can't fly a plane in.
And put a roof on it,
So you can't even get in with a rocket ship.
And don't put any windows or doors on it;
That's very important.

Build your Wall like this,
And none of "them" will ever, ever, ever, ever, ever, ever, ever, ever,
ever, ever, ever, ever, ever,
Be able to get in,

And, more importantly,
None of us will ever be able to get out.

Megan Baldrige

Pulling the Wall Over Our Eyes

During the campaign
we were curious,
about **that wall**!

Was the poorer, impecunious pais
really
purloining pockets
pressing public piggybanks for pesos,
robbing Pedro
to pay Paul,
putting up <u>someone else's</u> wall?

Our putative
president pipe-dreamed:
"Yes, *they will* pay
for our wonderfully
       big-league wall!"

We wall-wonderers,
asked,
"Why would Mexico
purchase a
pricey wall?"

"Of course,
they will pay!",
repeated the wall-et bearer,
post-truthfully
powerfully, pursing his lips.

But Mexico
did not say,
"Si, señor,
our bankers want to
build your wall."

Our prez persevered,
promising,
"They will pay"—

whilst whacking weakling past presidents—
for woeful wall laxity.

He drew a neon-red line
in the sand.
We circled the blinding line,
examined shifting grains:
was it a real line in real sand?

Or was it alternative-facts sand?
Was the line
red-state vermilion,
red herring carnelian,
or not-to-be reread, fading unred?

We deconstructed the wall:
could it really end opioids
in Iowa,
protect Maine from meth,
as our wallish president projected?

We searched
for clues
in the **un**failing,
indefatigable
New York Times.

From every angle
the wall was wallet-exploding,
not the common cure for
prescription drugs AND
bad hombres!

We knew people who knew people
who warned, "Watch his hands:
Is he putting the wall
into air quotes?"

They weren't buying
the trumped-up
Trojan horse
he hyped, as hope,
for the heartlands.

Mr. President,
no more pretending, please.
A complexity of
urgent needs
awaits your attention.

How about infrastructure repair:
fixing bridges,
highways,
elderly airports?
more drug rehab programs?

A wall of debt?
That: we do not need.

Kenneth Gurney

Hashtag

If Trump gets his wall built
I resolve to go visit the wall
where it stands along the Rio Grande
from Matamoros to El Paso
and push it over on its side
to form a fifteen hundred mile long
welcoming bridge.

If I hear you say, Kenneth
you are not strong enough to push over a wall
to span the Rio Grande,
I will smile, because I know
every American who thinks the wall
is stupid and useless
with hashtag push-it-over
will come and help me.
This includes the tin-starred border guards
who pine for their south-side view
and vacationers from Toronto
and Vancouver and other points far north
like Hammerfest Norway.

Joshua Gage

Tupilak in Cantaloupe Southern Diplomacy

A wall that they know for certain areas,
up so fast your head. We're going to build that
serious wall. Just remember we're going to
build going to build a wall to happen.
They know it wall. That wall will go but
in certain areas, a wall will spin. We are going to
wall. Mexico is going to just climb up,
and it's going to be a real border, and we're going to
be a real to build it. Don't worry. Fencing
is going to build a wall. You know we're going to
build a wall, folks. We're going to. It's going to
happen. Going build a wall. We're going pay
for the wall. Right? Strong. We are going to know,
you see, that they would build a fence. Construction.
It could be some. I know it. We are all good at this.
It's called is more appropriate. I'm very
to have borders nice and wall. I'm not going to say it....
It's going to that. And you remember, I'll be a serious wall.

Georgia Santa Maria

I Found a Golfball on the Border

I found a golfball on the border
The American dream in white

I found a golfball on the border
A mourning dove cooed nearby

I found a golfball on the border
By Asarco's belching pipe

I found a golfball on the border
Where the desert meets the tide

I found a golfball on the border
Where work is called a blight

I found a golfball on the border
And I thought we'd lost our sight

I found a golfball on the border
Definitions fit too tight

I found a golfball on the border
And I saw the other side

I found a golfball on the border
Where the bridegroom meets his bride

I found a golfball on the border
Where the desert sun wears white

I found a golfball on the border
By a river no one can find

I found a golfball on the border
The mountains displayed their spine

I found a golfball on the border
Where the stars shine cold at night

I found a golfball on the border
Some played, while others died

I found a golfball on the border
And I knew they all had lied

III.

Jules Nyquist, *Jornada del Muerto*

Eleanor Grogg Stewart

Do You Have a Secret?

Do you panic a little when you fill out a form
        and come to the one question
        you can't answer either way

Do you worry that the wrong person
        will notice your accent
        and guess what you're hiding

Do you want to work and study
        pay taxes and vote
        more than anyone knows

Do you dream that it will be better one day
        and that you can hang on till then
        and not be called illegal anymore

Do you have a secret?

Robbie Sugg

Passage

no fatherland
but souls
of the feet

no homesickness
but for darkness
behind eyelids

drought strikes
the savannah flashes
a mirage

my country
is a fence
crossing itself

Jennifer Maloney

Fort Worth, February 2017

Once,
they had to work
at indifference.

Once,
when the body fluids streamed, pooling
in the street
or in their shirtcuffs,
drying in their hair--once,
it was difficult
to be hard.

When they tied her wrists
and ankles,
she moaned,
not able
to lift her eyelids
in the bright Fort Worth sun.

When they strapped her on the gurney,
lifted her pale, bleeding weight
(light, very light)
into the running van--

When they slammed its doors
against the screaming
and the sobbing
of doctors, lawyers, husband, children--

By then,
it was easier.

They are not monsters, after all.

They go to church,
pay taxes, volunteer
play with their children,
tuck them into bed.

Once,
their work was hard.
but now their yoke is easy,
and their burden,
light.

>	Everything is possible
>	 under
>	a Great White God

Gretchen Schulz

refugee

yellow leaf flutters
sparrow's wings flail
falling towards nothing
on a refugee's trail

old dog mesmerized
caught in dark stare
while refugees rock rubber
boats going nowhere

some people own houses
three thousand feet or more
children with no blankets
sleep on a cold forests floor

yellow leaf flutters
sparrow's wings flail
falling towards nothing
on a refugee's trail

Steve Ausherman

Lengthening Shadows

In a province where structures are shaped
    From unfired adobe brick and straw
There fly the birds of Border Patrol pickup trucks
    Whose white flanks reflect like magpie wings
Their movements across the caramel floor
    Of a desert stitched with cactus and arroyo.

Their tires kick up dust tongues that spread out
    And form hands that build and mold
Great metal walls that stand steady from horizon
    To horizon like a fallen and stiff giant.
Metal looks foreign and uncertain in the desert.
    Barbed wire coils are the only circles to be seen.

In a province where structures are shaped
    From unfired adobe brick and straw
People seek freedom like hermits seek silence.
    Trails are made by javelina, fox and antelope,
Refugee and field mouse, ATV and truck.
    The desert has always revealed her wounds.

Truck tires kick up dust tongues that spread out
    Like a blanket covering two countries.
There is freedom in the heart of the desert.
    It beats with the rhythm of searching feet.
Of hands that grasp and won't let go.
    In the desert, the sun casts long shadows.

Lori Nolasco Martinez

The Children Who Were Stopped on the Banks of the Rio Bravo

(pastiche on Ingrid Jonker's "The Child Who Was Shot Dead by Soldiers at Nyanga")

The children who were stopped on the banks of the Rio Bravo
know that Honduras is no place for children
did they hear the screams
of their sister
gang-raped by youths who were once her classmates?
did they know she fell unconscious
after the third one took her?
did they hear the drunken chorus
and smell the bitter blood?

The children who were stopped on the banks of the Río Bravo
know their land is under siege
did they see their father's throat
slit by drug-dealing warlords?
did they hear his screams too
and smell the bitter blood?

The children who were stopped on the banks of the Río Bravo
sleep with one eye open in San Pedro Sula
neither the Mara Salvatrucha nor the Barrio 18 will butcher them
nor will they be massacred in Pradera del Sur
as like their brother they refuse to join the ranks
did they see him lying in the street
with a bullet in his head?

These children are the shadow of the soldiers
without a battlefield on guard with rifles and grenades
these children peep through the windows of houses where mothers barricade themselves
the children who just wanted to play in the sun at San Pedro Sula
are everywhere
the children who want to become men and women flee to the banks of the Río Bravo
will they ever become giants who travel through the whole world

Without borders?

Celeste Helene Schantz

A Database of Exhumed Objects to Identify Those Who Perished

Fluted skeletons of migrant children lay stacked
like bleached driftwood, or like kindling.
We disinter their bones; note incisions: evidence
of animal gnawing. Measure tapered ivory knuckles,
slender as crocuses, pushing up through the soil.

El Norte, Jim Hoggs County, Tepeguaje . . .
two kids tried to sneak around border patrol
check points. They have names, but we don't know
them. We say Case 408, Case 409.

Note one dirty baseball cap, Rangers royal blue, size small.
In situ, one stuffed orange lion, red rosary beads in a plastic
7/11 bag. We come to El Coyote Ranch, this paltry creek,
this field; to resurrect the relics of our disappeared.

Note the adamant husk of horse chestnut, green yarn.
A patch of blue sky that evening. Fresh cherry candy smile.
The stench of rotting Yucca; the 10-year-old boy's grimace,
the dark rise of stacked crates. The way his sister jumps
to the sand, sings Rihanna's Diamantes.

Of course, you must try to keep a clinical distance;
try to burn away the peripherals
of this mountain snow, these stars. Do not
imagine the girl's tousled hair as she whispers,
with parched lips, the names of your village saints,
or sights the blurred robin that flew over their heads
in the dusk: do not regard the binary of Gemini rising
over the plateau as armed shadows run toward them.

But tell me, you, who sit in your armchair: on your
life's last night, when the thing that sidles in on soft
and padded feet finally carries you away in its mouth—
Will the little children greet you? For, if you listen closely,
even now, far away, you can hear them calling your name.

They have names, but we don't know them.

We say Case 408, Case 409.

Sylvia Ramos Cruz

Give Me Your Tired
> *"your poor, your huddled masses yearning to breathe free…"*
> The New Colossus by Emma Lazarus

Sunday morning after our friends' marriage in *Ciudad Juárez, Méjico*, three of us and hundreds more—native, naturalized, alien—inch 1.9 miles, bumper to bumper for three hours to cross the Bridge of the Americas into El Paso.

At first, it's a *fiesta*—din of polychrome people carrying blanketed bundles north and south along the chain-link covered sidewalks. Never-ending stream of cars and trucks waiting obediently to file a foot or two. Snapping slap of international boundary flags. Vendors hawking news, *chicle*, corn, *Coca-Cola*, wooden puppets. Children crying to get a toy or drink; crying to get out and run around or just go to the bathroom. But, as minutes petrify into hours, the spectacle cannot alleviate the tedium nor stem the outrage that rises at the injustice of people penned and herded like *ganado* to the single gate where our fates await.

At last, we reach the Easy-Pass Lane gate; find we can't pass—three unarmed gray-haired American citizens deemed suspicious by militarized border guards. Maybe I shouldn't have greeted them *en español*. When searched, my kiwi green Ford Escape Hybrid disgorges contraband—one tiny live plant given to us as traditional Mexican wedding-guest favor, and one moribund Las Cruces motel-breakfast-buffet apple trying to sneak back into the homeland. They are conscripted; we are waved on home.

Finally north of *la frontera*, I breathe easy, wonder about others crossing the bridge. Were they walking away or walking toward? Had they ever stealthed through the night desert— shadowless, tremulous, silent— footsteps muffled by sand, erased by wind…

>ancient ritual
>caravan of hopes and fears
>our huddled masses

>hand punches sky
>through jagged hole in truck's roof—
>impatient young man

October breeze
mottled leaves fly in and out
free to cross borders

Neil Young

Window-seat on Eurostar

Just as my wee daughter nods off
in the pillow of my lap – we'll soon
be there at Disney, ssh!
the train jolts to a violent stop,
I gaze on what I knew was there
but hadn't thought would be
so panoramically displayed:
walled-up fields outside Calais.
I've strolled through fields like this before
– hedgerow paths and rights-of-way –
drowsed on trains as sunlit greens
refracted through the window
at my tired, day-dreamy eyes;
but here the segregation fence
hacks off the roll of scenery
much like those walls I've seen before
from west Belfast to Bethlehem
that go by names their makers call
peace line and security tower.
And I'm reminded, as by-passer,
what my window-seat is party to
even as I think 'what if
she wakes to see that view?'

Beyond that wall are children too,
the destitute of shared address;
we call it Jungle, as if they
are remade less human by the word.
Home has gentler tones for us
who greet it daily from our work
so we can travel tourist-class
with hard-currency passports;
though even here we're atomised,
there is no us, we incubate
detachment by unspoken norms,
we codify our separateness
as if we know that what we lack
can stay anaesthetised if held within;
it's how we filter out the news
of children sleeping wet in shacks –

the drowners on the heaving boats –
from those we hug to us.

That wall that breaches earth and grass
to brutish ethnic quarantine
affirms itself between us, our complicit solipsism;
we gawp behind headrests that serve
to camouflage our awkwardness
while uniformly pointing to
our singular, common route.
It's only minutes but my girl
is roused, the guard's apology
in French and English
offers ritual, reassuring words;
the Jungle turns to haze of grass,
I stroke her sleepy head,
deflect my useless guilt
resolved 'we'll never travel
down this route again.'

Craig Czury

The Border Crossing

I am at the border crossing waiting for the guard. I have my passport and my privilege stamped 1951. I'm at the border crossing waiting for the guard. I have my good looks and correct English. Charming. I'm at the border. At the crossing. I have my hands at my sides and my shoulders straight. I'm at the border crossing waiting with my white teeth and full head of hair. At the border, I'm at the crossing. 5:05. The watch.

Douglas Lipton

Birling Carrs

First, it's on the flowing tide
on the sand that we see her,
naked skin dark in the surf,
belly down, dragging herself
blubbering ashore, hopeful.

We walk towards her
to gawp or to offer succour,
take a camera shot,
make eye contact with eyes
that would stop the heart.

She drags herself away
back to the sanctuary
of the welcoming waves
as she loses herself
in the undertow.

An hour later, the tide is up,
and she is on the shelving rocks
this time, trying to lie low,
but when she moves her limbs
on the seaweed, we see her.

Again, we approach - to ogle,
maybe to help, but she'd
bite the hand, and how
would she feel – alarmingly hot,
wet, heavy – were we to lift her?

And who would want her
damaged skin, alien,
one of her kind in our midst?
What does she want here with us?
– they'd ask. Why here? Why us?

August 2015

Wayne Lee

Migration

Her Mexican works the garden
inside the deer fence, digs out
Scotch broom and blackberry roots.
Clean white t-shirt, rubber boots,
thick brown arms in the Easter sun.

He shows up once a year asking
for work, and he works hard,
never takes a break. She lends him
gloves and tools, provides breakfast,
bottled water, sack lunch.

Overhead, Canada geese fly north
on their migration, returning
to where they first pecked through
that thin, white shell
that once kept them safe.

The Mexican pulls off his gloves,
wipes his brow on a shirt sleeve,
looks up. Curse or prayer —
it's hard to tell for one
who does not speak his language.

Leah Zazulyer

Bitter at Her
                         In Jarabacoa, D.R.

Her Mexican grandparents were migrant farm workers
before *settling out* near the Hayward trainyards
in the San Joaquin Valley where they bore many children.

> *(As a strawberry picker once told a PBS interviewer,*
> *all poor people have in life is their children.)*

One daughter took up with a Bolivian guy who left for good
when their only child, Vanessa, was not quite four.

Catholicism and school were this child's salvations until she was fifteen
when her mother had an illegitimate baby.

No, no, no her high school counselor said, do not drop out,
go to college,
major in accounting, your mother has made her own bed…

Some long story not told between Catholicism and
an Hispanic evangelical church, between rejecting
accounting and volunteering to serve Christ teaching math in the D.R.

Another long story between the untreated acne that
had pitted the sides of her classic Aztec face, but
becoming gradually, irrevocably, aware of her own beauty…

But her mother was *bitter at her.* so she prayed day and night
she would be forgiven by God for abandoning her little sister….

She wanted to live alone, at last, in the forests and rice fields
of the Samana Pennisula,
            numbering the stars and calling them all by name

but the evangelists insisted she share quarters for safety's sake
with an another female student five years younger.

She tried to be just her mentor, to care for her like a mother,
to be a friend, to cook for her-- but they became lovers.

Weeping...

She is bitter at her lover, harsh, even cruel. Day and night she prays
God to transform her with HIS love, HIS power, to save her from her
sin...

She weeps when others sing or raise their arms in rapture, especially
when they
wash her feet like they washed Christ's.

At lunch she saves the soft crunchy bones of scrawny
Dominican chickens
to give her darling little white Chihuahua.

Karin Bradberry

Pantoum for Ra'ad Lalqaraghuli

I don't know what to believe—
From Baghdad to Baltimore we fled.
No one wants you here. Terrorist leave!
Reads the note we find – a new price on my head?

From Baghdad to Baltimore we fled
Seeking safety for our children, not
The note we find. The old price on my head
Ended in Iraq with my three brothers shot.

We seek safety for our children, not
Threatening notes tacked to the door.
Had home ended in Iraq, three brothers shot
So my children could fear still more?

Threatening notes tacked to our door
Remind us of the bullets and bombs
My children still fear, every day more—
I want to stay, but I'm having qualms.

Reminding us not of bullets and bombs
Our neighbors bring yet another surprise—
I want to stay, but I'm having qualms
Despite their fruit baskets and pumpkin pies.

One neighbor brought the first surprise:
No one wants you here. Terrorist leave!
Now baskets of fruit and pumpkin pies—
I don't know what to believe.

> **Note:** Written in response to *a New York Times* article November 14, 2016: "Refugees Discover 2 Americas: One That Hates, and One That Heals"

Lyn Lifshin

Life in Aleppo

a day without bombs,
is good. You can
leave your apart-
ment, wander thru
small oasis of color
and light. No words,
only the sense of
loss. No color except
for an plot of green
and one plum tree,
not turned to drift
wood. One man who
has not left, says you
must live on the lower
floors to try to escape
airstrikes, shells, rockets,
phosphorous bombs,
cluster bombs. Dreams
blend with nightmares,
ghosts rise from the ruins.
Stark white bones litter
the streets. No more
dancing, no more violins.
No flamingos or pelicans.
Terror blooms under a
blue moon. When a small
bomb lands on top of
a building, it often takes out
just the top 2 or 3 stories.
Lately Basha al-Assad and
the Russian military have
been using a new kind of
bomb that demolishes the
whole building. People
stay out of any rooms near
the street. There's no electricity.
Families rarely leave the apart-
ment, prefer to die together

Lyn Lifshin

When the Borders Close

people stow away,
slip through
black water
at night.
It is like a hike
through black leaves,
everyone together
in a clump.
My parents had a
three-year-old baby girl.
Everyone was taking hold,
caring for each other.
Wet birch and maples.
Whispering
under a blood moon.
Then the Germans
ambush
as the boat pulls out:
the child
held by her blonde hair—
a sneering tall Gestapo,
his knife against
her wet face

Lori Nolasco Martinez

Millennial Census-Taker
               (in response to Robert Frost's "The Census-Taker")

In lilac time I came to the Avenida
to that high-rise that bears the flame tree's name.
Doors left ajar to tantalize and torture
with subtle aromas of cilantro and bell pepper–
how many seasons until they're thrown open wide?
Who dwelled in each compact, box-like apartment
from which faint strains of salsa reached my ears?
I came as census-taker to my pueblo
not to count souls but to be counted amongst them.

What kind of errand is this when I knock
on strangers' doors? What emptiness, what hope?
Dwellers show themselves through chinks and gaps and cracks.
At least if they hid I could say that I found none.
Doors left ajar are worse than those that slam
and seal shut, secured by locks and deadbolts
while those within ignore the knocking and grow quiet.

The time was spring and the first rains of May
caused even the lilacs to shiver on the bush.
My boots made tracks and impressions on the still-
muddy ground but not the tracks I'd hoped for.
Then children who knew no evil or suspicion
appeared at the windows until their mothers called them
and jerked them back while the curtains billowed.
¡Vengan por acá, no estamos! We're not home!

Where is my portion of *pernil, mangú* and *flan*?
Who started this endless game of hide-and-seek
where even the children hide now in plain sight?
And what of breaking bread with guests and strangers?
I am no stranger nor am I a guest.
More than a stepmother, less than a child with birthright
I wait in joyful hope for the second coming.

Who will find the census-taker and count her amongst them?

John Macker

Navigating an Archipelago of Treacheries

The poppies are electric orange and bright as the sun. The wild roses climb up the wall into the sky. They bunch together in a refuge of fake, fallen stars that rustle restlessly in the May breeze. It is summer somewhere south of here. I can feel it coming, its wild breath in my face, warming without reassurance, on its trek from the borderlands to the high country.

In Mexico the journalists are disappearing like virgas, no trace of their words touching ground. This is where sacrifice has become bloody ritual, where each daily breath is caught in the act of gasping for prayer. The overheated silence replaces the words and the pages are worn by the wind into shreds, emptied of all meaning and the killing continues.

I want a reverie of last beers with Luis-Alberto Urrea and Charles Bowden.

I want to guide my aging bones into the desert walking until it becomes a wisdom tradition. I want to feel the heat of the sun on the back of my arthritic neck. I want to be accompanied by a corona of hummingbirds. Out here the border trekkers navigate an archipelago of treacheries and burnt-out days without succor or shade. We are coming for them but they are not waiting for us. We will freeze them in their tracks at the wall that somebody around here with circumspect knowledge of the issue is going to pay for. We will stop them in their paw prints. We will plunder animal and plant families and separate them from themselves. The coming heat and the purity of our mission will be relentless and without remorse.

In a reverie I'm blasting back midnight beers with Urrrea and Bowden. I am drinking for the lost souls and the misbegotten, my bleeding heart lunges at shadows, won't let me sleep, calls me foul names. Like many people, I used to save all this self-sabotage for the duskiest ends of the day. When I could hear the desert age and then renew itself in the rhetorical flourishes of songbirds. In the ascetic ramblings of the scorpion. When the scent of it was shamelessly spring blossom sweet.

Lawrence Welsh

Rio Grande Roadrunner

forgive eyes
that become mexico
or the border patrol's
glassed intent beyond
the water.
out here
all appearances
disappearances
can whisper
or shout:
i am the line
an escapee
of the blue sky
desert aire
and fall or rise
for some resurrection
like a new palette
or canvas cleansed
by the freedom
of a scrubbing
of a washing
the taunts of some
to jump
to rush
to complete a loca's
or local's dare

John Macker

On the Borderline with Pancho Villa

(for Lawrence Welsh)

My famous river's edge
   cottonwoods
over one-hundred years old
are almost skeletons now
brittle deep roots in the worn hallowed ground
quenched by the medicine
of time's passage.
This is where our borders come
to pray against prayer
to grieve against grief

We're close enough to touch the
tragedy of Mexico
with our ghost fingers,
ascendant moon illuminates this ancient
fabric of space,
where the last revolution's
blue heron lifted off the Rio Grande
and once the smoke cleared:

where the blood reached deep ground
towards a new inventory of darkness.

John Roche

The Backpack

"A young black man about 16 is roaming the neighborhood.
He has a backpack."

Someone posted this to my neighborhood watch app.
Last week it was a pack of coyotes roaming the neighborhood,
eating kittens and small dogs,
but this is much worse.

What is in his backpack?

Maybe it's a bag of drugs to corrupt the kindergarteners.
Maybe it's a bag of burgler's tools.
Maybe it's three sticks of dynamite.
Maybe it's a human head.
It better not be a book bag.
There's nothing worse than Reading While Black.

Yes, it is a book bag
He has a book in it
He has a pencil
He has a notebook
He may even have a laptop!

O Holy Trump,
Save us from this dangerous boy.
Deport him, we pray!

Tina Carlson

Deportations

1.
What we call alien
is three parts water, one
part prayer. Lucinda, dig deep
into your reliable rivers
of blood. Your red dress
a flame in me. The world
mirrored with our likeness.
How your grandmother
conversed with the
whispering trees,
taught you fire, electron,
retina, marrow.

2.
Forests are set ablaze
and turned to soot.
Mud and bone make
agreements that the
small boy who flees
his own father
becomes bird, tree.

3.
Alert with hawk call,
yesterday's wind dropped
branches, pod flags
still pulsing on the ground.

4.
On my fever pillow:
small cots suspended
from dreams of trees
where children toss and cry
out, the not-yet-found or sent-
into-exile. Moon's headlamp
shines on bark scarred from
drought and fire, alert with
underground messages.

O breeze-blown, blend our
lives into light and sap
that the edicts and armies
might pass us by.

Scott Wiggerman

Some of Them Were Dreamers
(a golden shovel incorporating an Issa haiku)

Hard rain knocks blossoms
to earth. I watch at
a window till night

overruns the day, and
still no end to the
torrent's playlist. Border faces
peek from other windows: the dread of
isolation, the need for people

through the deluge. I have not moved,
immersed in blossoms mashed by
indifference, bled of all music.

Bart White

My Brother's Keeper

Soup's the theme for this poem—
you may think it unworthy,
but this is really good soup
our waitress has brought and set before us
on the counter where we like to sit,
my daughter and I, in the village diner.
Chicken noodle for me, minestrone for her.
Steam rises in happy tendrils
from two white bowls with a square pack
of crackers tucked beside.
On paper napkins as on a cloud
silver moon-faced spoons made for this moment.
Everything as it should be.
I bend to take the first taste.

I know the world suffers, its sorrows
are renewed each day—they're in my pocket
on the phone I carry— its black screen
springs to life with a swipe of a finger.

We eat our soup, open the crackers and dip them.

Children cross our borders under cover of night.
We don't know what to do with them.
By the thousands they have come.
We are appalled: what mother would send
her child on such a journey?

We slurp our soups, trade tastes.

Seven-year old Arturo is looking for his brother
who didn't come home last night.
The abandoned building at the end of this street
is where bad things happen, but that's where his brother must be.
Lookouts see him walking as one to an execution.
These watchers of the street watch him and are silent.

Arturo pauses at the doorless threshold.
He calls into the darkness.
No one answers.

He steps inside.

I think and do not think
        of the boy gone to seek his brother.
Of the two sets of clothes—the jeans,
two t-shirts, one bigger, one smaller
on a bed they shared in a simple room.
Or of their mother who lay them side by side
on the bed, smoothing the clothes
with the palm of her hand
again and again.

We have finished our soups; our bowls are empty.
the goodness of the soup is inside us.

I give my gracias for the blessing of the soup.
I ask forgiveness that I am not my brother's keeper.
I beg perdono, and in the name of Arturo,
I pray.

Mary Strong Jackson

Dear Mexican Friend

let's cross real and imagined walls
write words of moon-gazing lives
until stanzas streak with strands of gray
and each day becomes a poem
we'll feel the effort of the pen
against our palms   the climb out of our beds
the way our knees pop   your right   my left
the less than fresh eyes   every line and bag
will accentuate our mirrored reflections
as we smirk in camaraderie
never denying joy coiled through pain

even in darkness our minds enter realms
of light and idea not yet sculpted or written
every night   you in Mexico
me in America   will chase our thoughts
like tortoise and hare for what-if routes
and unlit fires   we will drift to sleep
with thoughts of bills   children   doubts

by morning our minds might inhale true clichés
of today's blessings   we'll greet the regulars
at the coffee shop writing their own lives
each with real or imagined pen poised
as they write the stories of their lives

Jules Nyquist

Imaginary Borders

We are tourists and U.S. Citizens driving on New Mexico
Highway 22 towards the Tent Rocks
when a ROAD CLOSED sign surprises us.
A U.S. Immigration Border Patrol station spans the road
behind a detour sign.
We drive around and notice "Mexico" on the other side
in red, green, and white.

How is this possible?
It must be a movie set, the only explanation we can think of.
We are near Pueblo de Cochiti
crossing pueblo land, government land,
private land, sacred land.

We drive the gravel road
climbing precarious curves to the top of the mesa
and I wonder if the gray clouds in the distance
will bring rain and flash floods
leaving us stranded.
The overlook is named for American Veterans
and we walk the loop trail
while lightning flashes make me uneasy.

Am I trespassing in this place of indescribable beauty?
Volcanic ash piles from eons ago hold songs
from the women of Cochiti, the storytellers.
They echo through the spirals
preserve lost heritage.

On our drive back we approach a red pickup truck
Stopped in the middle of the gravel road.
We wait awhile, then move to pass.

The woman is praying, she tells us through her open window.
We know now we can stop being tourists.

On our pretend entry out of Mexico,
we are free to return to Albuquerque
unlike the thousands who try to cross that border daily
unlike the real wall building into something unimaginable.

Stuart A. Paterson

News

Today I thought I ought to write a poem
about how borders heave with refugees,
weave metaphors like plaited grass,
give voice to untranslated pleas.
Last week it should've been
a poignant tribute to the lives lost
in a migrants' boat which sank
off Sicily, that earthquake
in Tibet, another suicidal middle
eastern market square attack.

I think those poems, type them out
in brain fluid, print them off in breaths
reserved for sympathy which does no good.
On Portling beach the morning tide
has left a memory of person,
a tragicomic skeleton perched
wistfully on the skerries looking out
to England, wide-eyed, open-mouthed
as if warning everybody in the south,
the world, of sudden spates, lost balance, last
ones for the road, red-lettered bills,
missed calls, inactions, life-defining sanctions,
border crossings that will never pass
& ultimately, of being late.

The week is crammed with awful news.
At least, from here, there are stunning views.

skerries – coastal rocks

IV.

Kevin Zepper, *Chaco*

Pamela Williams

Destructive Construction

We build them ourselves, you know.
Oh, possibly some guidance from a racist father,
or frightened grandmother
who lived through a time
when there was really *not* enough.
Having read the story
of that compassionate judge
who spent the night
sharing the cell and the fear
of the vet with ptsd, and claustrophobia,
after doing the required sentencing…
He talked him back to the embrace
of the southland,
They communed in meatloaf and humanity.

How did we become so lost, so disparate
from one another,
and still so very much the same?
Reaching for trust in our intentions,
straining to raise the vibrations
for all the hungry ghosts.
You could never exhaust such abundance,
not in another foolish lifetime.
I discover myself weeping
again, and again,
broken open most often
by the stories of crumbled walls.

Colleen Powderly

Jo Almost Despairs

Standing astride Seneca Lake Jo surveyed farms and towns, houses with barbeques in back, barns where cows called for milking in the evening light. Tiny cars rushed on roads the width of her bootlaces. A Mennonite carriage traced its slow route home past a prison caged by high fences and razor wire, white deer dotting the surrounding woods. By her instep a car turned out its drive, drove a mile or so, and stopped. A woman hung her head out the window transfixed by a gold dot which, while she and Jo stared, became a golden eagle lifting up over the trees. The woman scrounged a pencil stub and paper, scribbled a poem on the spot. Jo smiled—crazyass poets still lived.

Patricia Roth Schwartz

Hat Poem
                (at Auburn Correctional Facility)

From a skein of pale green yarn
and a plastic hook, Poppi's making
a hat. He's so good now he doesn't
even look as hat or scarf or shawl
grows and grows, billowing down
in strips from the dipping, hooking
tool that's got a rhythm of its own now,
like poems. Poppi's making a hat while
he and Chris and Sundiata sit in the back
of crochet class and compose triptych poems
they'll warble out later in poetry class. How
lucky they are and lucky they know it
to get these scant chances here in Hell or
Oz or whatever you want to call it, to meet
and sit and learn to make something to keep
a loved one they can't touch or see warm
on a walk they can't take, then to stand, belt
out their own precious words, hooked
together, before the group we've started
to call family, home, Holy Ground.
Poppi's making a hat.

M. J. Iuppa

Next Time

If I knew the precise hour that's natural
as uncertain weather, that's neither winter

or spring, but something that insinuates
itself in a blank sky, I would be guilty of

living detached yet watchful of a wall that
casts its shadow in the light we've gained

by forfeit of sleep. I would be caught
looking up into sky's vastness— its twilight

gloaming over this landscape, as if it were
searching for its lost twin—the one we

opened up to without fear of being left on
a stranger's doorstep—the one who

promised us providence in a remote hour.
If only we could hold on to that instant

of weather that spins us dizzy in wind's
brisk interrogation, we wouldn't be

caught off-guard, or without words
to scale down this wall's provisions

that will never protect us.

Maril Nowak

Light and Dark: A Synthesis

Spectral as dark angels
in a shimmer of dark shingle
over pleats of earth and cornstubble
windows of the floodlit country
church permit no light.

the way a big brother gawps
slack-jawed as Death clutching
a flashlight underneath his chin
to make the night grow deeper
nostrils and eye sockets

the way we know some evil
by the vowel it sings forever out
the way a synthesizer's vox angelica
oo-ahs out and out not pausing for
the slightest human gasp and

held my throat until I caught the joke
of it that choked me back to reason.

Nathanael William Stolte

All the Screens Between Us

I read an article in
Time about the
mental health issues
associated with
social media

specifically
how it's affecting
young people

there is a new
kind of human
suffering

garnered by
modernity

a wall of the mind
a border war
a blight of convenience

brought upon us by
all the screens between us

Steven Deridder

Don't ever forget

You didn't have a care in the world.
You never worried about the playpen,
or the picket fence,
or the four dry walls that boxed your room.

When you were outside, that's where you were.
You weren't looking down on a cell phone.
You laid your dewy eyes on everything.
Wonder wasn't a trial.

When someone asked your opinion on something,
you were only concerned about why they asked.
When someone hated someone else or only cared about
specific bullshit, like family or friends or color or creed,

you didn't understand it.
Why not care for everyone, for everything?
Stress isn't caring.
You never had a care in the world, caring for everything.

I guess that's what love is.
Love for life.

That didn't work out, though.
You grew up.
You realized
that without a wall

what would you climb?
There must be something
more,
you thought.

Karin Bradberry

Standing for Your Name
                      (In remembrance of Bruce Palmer,
                              Vietnam Veteran)

I didn't expect to see your name,
a poet I often shied away from,
anger and pain you couldn't contain.

Though the VA often gets our blame
their memorial roll call was well run—
I didn't expect to hear your name.

No one was present to stand and claim
you - a fallen brother - succumbed
to the anguish you'd never contain.

The chaplain's words proclaimed
each one's worth without beating a drum—
I hadn't supposed I'd hear your name.

Your words were daggers, wounds inflamed
I wanted to read more than the sum
of all the hurt you couldn't contain.

A boy's simple card filled me with shame
Have a good life. Hope you do awesome.
I hadn't expected to stand for your name
or to feel the pain you couldn't contain.

Leah Zazulyer

Café, Cincinnati Airport

Overly solicitous kid waiter
recommends the quesadillas
and made-to-order chocolate chip
cookies--not as great as his mother's,
but darn good he says.

With servile civility he asks
how are things-- four times
more water, lemon-- three times
extra napkins-- five supplied
your flight on time?

Then I'm just back from Iraq
he says brightly, adding
he learned a lot and was glad
to serve his country in
a tech support van near Basra.

Combat I ask–
not really, except some wounded
in the field hospital, and my girlfriend
who promised her dying buddy
to tell his mother goodbye.

We are against the war I venture.
Well yeah, you know he says
crouching now beside our booth
as if taking cover in a fox hole,
in my poly sci class at junior college
our teacher used to say it was all about oil
and I listened real hard when Bush was running
that first time against--I forgot his name
but it was hard to figure, and
I finally decided every president wants the best
for his country, they just have different ways…

So, how're the cookies he asks,
its melted chocolate bleeding all over our hands,
my 26th birthday is coming up
and mom's promised to make me some
I can hardly wait.

Loren Niemi

Not the Date

It was not the date I expected
Nervous as I was that it might go
Well when we spent two hours

Talking death, cancer,
The strokes of friends, parents,
Grandparents with brain tumors.

Death is a border, politics is as well
The both of them marking of ends
Where passports mean little or everything.

All the while I was looking into
Her eyes wondering how we got to
This conversation out of the gate?

It looked like a kiss was not in
The offing as the dessert course
When her tears fell in the soup.

Mina Hatami

Closed Doors

Closed doors,
Damn closed doors
Line of dominos that don't fall

Kick the door open
And you reach the second door
Year after year
Day after day
Fighting the shut doors

Natural rebel
Yup, spending the whole life in a cage
                      Fighting everyday,
                                    Yup, natural rebel

The doors are all broken
The walls, down
Rubbles behind me
Delicious fresh air, ahead

Openness
        freedom
                ease
                          acceptance
Love
        passion
                elation
                        trembling
                                ecstasy
                                      desire
                                              All, for me

The air, for me
The breath, for me

The door, for you
The prison, for you
The name, for you

Life, for me
Mina, for me

Go to hell,
      for you!

Janet Ruth

Cage

What is it like?
inside a body that can no longer—
    smash the ball over the back fence
        and round third base for home with ease;
    hike up the Blue Mountains
        and return dragging a buck;
    power across the ice on silver blades
        and glide back gracefully in reverse.

What is it like?
inside a mind that can no longer—
    track the rules and progress
        of the Eagles football game on television;
    recall your favorite stories about years
        in Europe rebuilding houses and lives after the war;
    remember the words you sang
        to a six-year-old, "*You are my sunshine . . .*"
inside a mind that leaves you
    half-way through a task—
        confused—
            a hunting dog that has lost the scent.

I know that bearded young man
    with gold-rimmed glasses paces
        somewhere within.

There are so many questions I should have asked—
    how do I live a life of integrity
        in a shattered world?
So many things I should have told you—
    I am proud of your example;
    I love you even though we clashed—
        two deer locking antlers.

But I was too stubborn
    like you;
too unwilling to take the first step—
    like you?

Too young and busy
to recognize the drift of time.

Now I am here,
        a hacksaw blade hidden in my boot,
to slash through the bars of the cage—
        to let you out;
        to let me in;
or at least
to thrust my arm between the bars
        and seize your hand.

Jane Lipman

Extraterrestrial

She feels as exposed (sneaking
down a hospital corridor at 7 am
in a strapless evening gown—
a clump of doctors staring
like a luncheon of Hadassah women),

as though caught by extraterrestrial
police for spooning under
the four moons of Jupiter.

She and her lover, a medical
resident, hadn't thought about
this part the night before.

Looking for an unlocked door
she escapes,
inhales slowly,
takes in her heart's quiet.

Linda Yen

Therapy at the Healthplex

Hunched over the steel walker
your spine a wobbly crane
hoisting the ball and chain of your body

I pedal even harder as you pass by
surrender my thoughts
to the mind-numbing hum of the cardio machine

unsure if I should smile or engage you
in small talk, knowing you'd think my affliction
pales compared to yours.

I watch you grit your teeth
struggle against the idiot disconnect
of mind from body, while I mask the pains

flaming through mine, wishing I could say to you
listen, I've known it, I've felt it
how dreams can redeem you

how you can glide with the ease
of angels, riding the crest of clouds
far above the city

how, in the soul's ascension,
the body remembers its perfections
before it was wounded, before it was birthed

before it was tossed by fickle fate
into the steely clutches of pitiless infirmity.
But I won't, because I am afraid

You'd nod and avert your gaze
or scoff at the suggestion
when all I can hope for

all I can ask for, is you'd shut your eyes
and for one brief second
feel yourself rise in sun swept joy

fanned by the downy wingbeats
of that ghost bird, the Phoenix
hovering above us

in our dreams.

Margaret M. Baumler

Where Do Dreams Go?

Where do our dreams go?
(those creatures of our off-duty minds).
Capricious, they leave us in the land of sleep
but sneak upon us in our daytime state,
to be caught up in their scrambled associations.
Our arm and hand are raised up, holding back
a heavy lid, while our neck and head are bent,
scrutinizing a Pandora's box.
Where is Joseph now, we ask. It is not just
kings that seek interpretation.
Plagues beset the common soul and are heaped up
backwards behind the grey tissue.
But who can see their long-range implications?
(Perhaps a Solomon?) Is there a prophet in the house?
Were there days when the bridges could be raised
between these lands of awake and sleep?

We span the pons, we squint and tighten
the crevices of our face
as if to see with our eyes open
what we saw with our eyes closed.
We even affect altered states of consciousness
hoping to discover heavens in our mental perambulations,
or daytime clues in cloud formations.

Sometimes, we wander among Jack Frost's
fluted ferns as if on demi-feet we trod frozen
leaving not a curlicue askew.
We dance in a looking-trance with a gaping face.
Are we then near the limbo of aborted dreams?
Does the gem of our thoughts emerge here
frequently to be squashed down by that watch-dog part of our mind?
Who guides these newborn amphibians whose
flippers make futile little gestures
trying to swim again in Jung's sea of consciousness?
Quickly, they must go before the sun shines on their upturned bellies.
In vain, we would catch them, for as turtles turned they would tell us
nothing.

Alas, our sleuthing needs the fog that swirls and mists
before the mountain steep that flirts with bough and limb and trunk,
making for us a daydream netherlands
where our ancestors found the little folk.

Falling into that state is a curtain of velvet quietly slipping,
its folds scurrying across those baser urges
that caused us to put on our slippers
and walk asleep in our childhood.
Did we have then mere glimpses of the Helvetian brain?
—that our newer cells shudder and flinch at—
pierced as Ocdipus when he heard the news
or Freud when he figured it out.
They must be two, the old mind and the new
and calloused must be the fissure that grows between.

V.

John Roche, *City of Rocks*

Margaret Randall

Louder

Words shove their swollen fingers
through iron grates
where hastily added bars
render openings too small to show
a face absent of grimace,
a mouth closing about syllables
saying what they mean.

They are what we have left,
these words,
and daily the bully mouth
tries to reshape their purpose,
cut them to his size,
declare them fake or irrelevant
to the traps he lays.

Sticks and stones was the ditty
we learned in safer times
when papers of record and radio
believed in impartiality
and wholesale entrapment
was rare enough
to jar complacency.

The words themselves hold power
only on our courageous tongues,
between our teeth,
shot from makeshift slingshots
in our trembling hands.
Louder our hearts demand
as memory seconds the motion.

G. E. Schwartz

If There's a Wall

If there's a wall
there's going to be a way through: a
gate or door. There's going to be
ladders, yes, and also
sentinels who sometimes sleep.
There are going to be secret passwords you
can overhear. There will be methods
of torture for extracting clues
to maps of underground passages
complete with oxygen-lines and mini-scooters.
There will be drones, yes, drones,
improvised explosives, battering rams,
armies with Jericho-sized trumpets
whose unified blast will shatter
the foundations.

If there's a wall there will be
words to whisper by loose-mortar'd bricks,
great wailing prayers to summon, birds
to carry messages taped to their legs.
There will be texts texted— some
even forming poems.

Faint as in a dream
will be the voice that calls from the belly
of that wall if
there IS a wall.

Dennis Maloney

from Border Crossings, #4

A dictionary explodes sending words
fleeing towards the borders,
chased by those without name
toward a great unknown destination.

Words are refugees smuggled in hidden
train compartments, walking obscure paths
through farm fields, forests, washing
up dead on shores, lost at sea, crawling
under fences and over walls built to keep them out.

Words are on a clandestine voyage seeking asylum
in an unknown language, their passports thick from
collecting official stamps over centuries. One
can't overestimate the amount of accumulated baggage.

Dennis Maloney

from Border Crossings #5
                      (for Fouad El-Auwad)

The Syrian poet entered Germany at sixteen
and now reads his poems in both
the sonorous Arabic and the harder
German cadence. Both beyond my understanding.

After the poems come audience questions
not about the syntax of the poems
and their wild unpredictable lines
but the fractured country he left decades ago.
A country shattered into shards like
a precious porcelain Chinese vase
hitting the floor, hard. They ask
how can the mangled lives and broken
cities be put back together again?

What is the poet's answer? That
a storm is gathering over the world,
that there are no victories,
that we must learn not to be afraid,
that we all must learn to speak a new language.

Loren Niemi

Kabir on the Border

Here along the imaginary separation
Of the geo-politic
Each side looks alike
The dark shadows of water and pines the same
The clouds the same
The making love the same
Birth and death as ubiquitous

As the rising sun or moon
And so too the setting; all the same.
So too the turning of the season
Same air. Same blood.
Where is the border
Of this thing called country
in the midst of this sameness?

On the glacial pool I am reading Kabir
His words leap from 15th Century Persia
To speak of that other sameness;
Where he says spirit is a border seldom crossed
Though no visa is necessary
For consciousness.
Yet few travel that path.

His words cut the air sharp as the sound
Of mosquito wings
Startling the sleeper to wake.
Even when the mark of hunger's bite disappears
The knowledge of having been bitten
Remains under northern lights
A decaying afterthought of chilled waters.

I want to float on those waters
Sans motor. Sans boat.
Sans feasting insects. Sans body
Letting the heart float beneath the curtain of light
Like a dragonfly.
I want to soak in starlight and cross the borders
Of spirit to sing, statelessness.

Don Paul

Goodby, Walls

There are walls made up of numbers
Walls made of cards Walls made of code But no walls at all under Jesus' God
There are walls around Golf Courses
Walls around Streets Walls around Cays But no walls at all under Durga's God
There are walls made up of skin-tones Walls of fractions Walls of factions But no walls at all under Damballah
Imagine all those walls goners
Imagine all those walls Tesla
Imagine all those walls wild as Willies Imagine aged beauties of Villon and Hafiz Imagine flowers of O'Keefe
Imagine all those walls tossed into the Sky and Sea To celebrate Wisdom
In our God and our Gods.

Stewart S. Warren

When You Come Upon a Prisoner

"Do not disturb the mind
of the ignorant,"
the Italian Alchemist said
when speaking of spirals.

Bring hot soup and a blanket
to their cold cell, and though
you know the door is unlocked, ajar,
forcing the issue now
would only bring accusation of denial,
a face full of claws.
And what good would that do—
disobeying your first responsibility
to yourself, and provoking
another to commit a wrong?

When your work in town is done
come back to the forest, your circle here
among friends warming themselves
around the quiet flame, self-contained,
flickering in peaceful alliance.
Join the joyful. Tend the fire
a stick at a time.

One by one the astonished captives
come stumbling into camp.

Dwain Wilder

The Tiny House

This tiny house, fastened well,
small enough and sturdy to banish
all that is too large for exchange—
arguments about foundations,
taboos that bind life
into currency exchanged with friends, lovers,
politicians and the police.

Only tiny things will fit here
within the vacant windows—
love itself, always ready
for larger accommodations,
or even, tiny as it is,
the vast dreams of night
after a day in the sun where is needed
no refuge.

Mary Elizabeth Lang

Deconstructing "Mending Wall" (a variant sestina)

> *Before I built a wall I'd ask to know*
> *What I was walling in or walling out,*
> *And to whom I was like to give offence.*
> —Robert Frost

My student from Sri Lanka reads Frost in Connecticut
where irregular strings of stones dot the landscape.
She's seen granite faced, black hatted pilgrims
in history books. On the edge of a primeval forest,
they pried up boulders, balancing one on one
to wall out predators, wall in cows or wheat.

In other pictures, the landscape is peopled
with Indians living on the edge of the Quinnipiac,
fletchers of flint and feather, noble wall-builders,
rolling the boulders into intricate patterns
under a granite sky to appease Earth's spirit
so it will not send killing frost too soon.

I say to her, *Look back further, to the wall*
of granite-colored ice that melted, leaving
frosted stones to form Long Island and the Sound;
or further still, to the edge of a geologic age
that threw up boulders high enough to form
a landscape of Hanging Hills, Appalachia's tail.

In the shadow of a giant boulder, West Rock,
we sit in my windowless office, deconstruct landscapes
that cannot be seen from here. She says Frost
has seduced her to walk ragged walls in February,
brushing snow off makeshift granite benches
to sit on what she sees as civilization's edge.

Perched like a Sri Lankan parrot on that wall,
her flowered sari belongs in another landscape
where perfume of night blooming jasmine edges out
scent of sea wind, where smooth black boulders
of volcanic rock—not granite—confront the spray
that frosts the stone not with ice, but salt.

She thinks she'll find answers carved in granite,
but Frost still eludes her, piling up line on line
like boulders between himself and his sari-wrapped
neighbor from another land. Though he keeps the wall
between them, she shifts a stone at the edge of her brain
and totally rearranges the landscape around her.

Those who build or topple walls in her mind's landscape
are not humans or elves, but hoar-frost gods of granite,
striding the edge of the field, shouldering boulders.

Mary Dudley

On the birth of the Nigerian Twins

When Faith and Favour were lifted from their mother's womb,
they searched each other's face,
looked into one another's eyes
and saw the world.

Their bodies joined at the belly,
they shared their parts without regard
for what belonged to whom:
they sucked each other's fingers;
they stroked each other's cheek;
they often kissed.

Two months along and they were separated.
Seventeen surgeons,
specialists of every sort,
and nurses
transformed them into two.

What do they carry
in their inchoate memory
of their swim toward light?

Do their limbs remember
and long to wrap around the other's;
their hands still search the other's mouth?

Who is the other
that has come from one?
Is there incessant longing for reunion?

Is that what wakes us all at night
and makes us reach across to find
our other body-- to cup our other shoulder,
hip, or face.

Does each of us seeing through the glass
remember our other self?

Do we long for that time
when we knew that we were one?

Eleanor Grogg Stewart

The Walls of Time

(Dedicated to Than Trong Ai)

The walls of time are unclimbable
They are opaque as dirt and crumbly
They shift each time you touch them
And close again as you peer through
Only the markers you left as you built
Can be found and swept of mystery
Each of us lives ahead of our history
But a memory wall can sometimes fall
And a person from one's distant past
Walks through as if it were not there
A Vietnamese man from the 80s
In the refugee camp on Palawan
Flew through time to visit me here
He left a gift that sees through walls
The computer I'm using—and this
"You didn't only teach us English
You showed us how to live again"
I have done one great thing in my life
I thought it lost behind a wall of time
But Than Trong Ai broke through
And though the wall has risen again
And though my eyes are full of tears
He gave me the courage to write on
In these my few and final years

Randy Prus

*On Turner & Time, too**
                    (for Tim Boatmun, again)

....autumn lines settling
in springtime gardens...

...the last two lines, you say,
further the distance, an echo,
of what you once heard...

...sound hides itself in buildings,
waiting to be re-thought...
...spring occurred early, this year..

...a brick wall is a form of art..

...just as listening to footsteps
along a labyrinth, restores
music to the body, an echo,
of lives once heard...

...I've forgotten the return...

* Joseph Mallord William Turner, R.A.

Bruce Noll

A Time to Bring Stones Together

I have carried stones for walls
and for the sheer delight of
feeling their dead weight.

They didn't wiggle like
a fish to be free
but let me test their heft
to see if I could pry them away
from stagnancy.

Some were so set
in their ways they needed
prompting from a bar.

Stubbornness also has a
place in the way of things.

Bruce Noll

Builders

Give a moment to the
builders of a country
or any famous edifice.
It was not the politician,
business magnate or corporation
who constructed these.
Hadrian did not build his wall,
nor Eifel his tower.
The plaza in New York was not
built by a Rockefeller.
No president or emperor
ever made a country.

It was laborers
who laid the stone and concrete,
set tiles in Roman cities
or your own bathroom,
masons who carved the stone for cathedrals.
Steel workers put up skyscraper
skeletons, was they who made the ships
that carried supplies, carpenters
and bricklayers who caused walls
to rise in towns and cities.

We give mayors' names to buildings,
chewing gum or catsup titles
to arenas but somewhere
under beams, scrawled on inner walls
are written signatures of workers
who wanted to be remembered.
They are the ones who crushed their fingers,
went home with aching backs and limbs,
mixed real blood and sweat into their work.
Whether you walk an ancient cobbled street,
ride on rails or six lane highways
give a thought to those who gave you
shelter, peace of mind and comfort.

Renny Golden

Magicians
                    (1836, Illinois and Michigan Canal)

We come from Connemara farmers
who carried stone to the sea, our arms
broke bog's rock walls.

This is the river we Paddies run
to the big hound Mississippi.
Our arms slice prairie, hardpan and black root.

We, the anonymous, caked in dirt.
Bruised hands gut meadows of canary weed,
sedge marsh alongside dark men with scarred

backs, lashed by a deeper servitude.
Together worn down, our shoulders cramped.
We open thirty miles of glacial till,

men, as taken for granted as this canal
turned backwards, pierced with locks
and pumping stations. Our young lives

save a city from typhoid; make a way through
bedrock. We magicians do not
attend the "shovel-day" opening.

We are the nameless, who made
a silver highway for freight boats
pulled along tow-paths by mules like us.

Bill Nevins

Wind Fall

> *Don't ever change people even if you can*
> *Don't change before the empire falls*
> *You'll laugh so hard you'll crack the walls*
> —Jefferson Airplane, "Greasy Heart"

Must Fall
Should Fall
Will Fall

After that death,
we never saw
coming,
a death too soon
that wall
went up

that cursed Wall
so
we could not talk

Estranged. How strange.

That wall must fall

I throw love

throw love
over the wall
under the wall
through the wall

love through the air
love in the wind

wall fall
  wind will wash
wall fall
   wind will roar
wall fall
   wind will blow

love against the wall

love you all

keep on battering
down this Empire's wall

with love

until

There is No Wall.

Karla Linn Merrifield

Wherehow

Going bordering
testing our limits

canoe & paddles
on Rio Grande

Santa Elena
fatigues us with silt

no Border Patrol
nearby we border

on exhaustion
grow very thirsty

nothing illegal
in our slow thoughts

just making a bend
surely as turtles

nationality
quite unimportant

more shade desired
more water better

but canyon walls
mock us like ravens

we lumber along
elementally

between two countries
neither belonging

to tiring muscles
our wasting pink skin

we trespass the silence
without clear borders

in this sere land
accompanied by

thunder, clear warnings
to go downstream now

strokes before heat strokes
we must go homeward

but where, how

Mary Strong Jackson

On Both Sides of the Wall

clouds have shadows
making blues deeper
but the other way
the bluest way has the whitest clouds
it's about reflection
one thing bounces off another
the way space   the blackest black
has the most light unseen
until a hand in the dark
reflects   and then
the light!

Janet Eigner

Higher Math

I savor packing for days, sifting canyon memories from the lumpy
backsack. The faded down vest pulled from a stuff bag expands,
releases a few feathers— prisoners escaping, or seeds from
a pod feathering the desert air. Redrock grit chiaroscuros

the thrice-resoled boots. I count the plane miles to
Phoenix, a half-day stretch. The air cools on the
drive north, climbing from Saguaro and Organ
Pipe to Ponderosa. By late afternoon, I grope

for the compressed vest, feel it expand
around my chilly shoulders. In the
bracing South Rim sunset, then,

 metal and wheels and cares
finally shed, I am planted
and can no longer count
the salutations bestowed

by this universe revealed
through pulsing feathers
of fog. Flesh of the rock,
Shekhinah and Kachinas,

the Everything in the
brilliant Void.
The Half and the
Other Half.

Janet Eigner

On the Way Down

I expect welcome and pleasure here
in this six-million-year-old cradle

so solidly rooted in knobby pink granite
and slabbed gray schist.

I am home. Here I know what I am.
My bootprint won't last like the ancient footprints

or the headressed shamans, antelope, spirals,
rain signs chinked and carved in this redwall.

Thick mist on our descent shrouds the familiar mesas
but pain quickly clears my view and I am rent.

Like the boulders we pass, house-large
once hurtled down the canyon walls

husks of me cleave away—as chaff down a chasm—
long blindness to what boils within,

like the volcano's magma
that once flowed, then hardened beneath my feet,

like the sheer, icy torrent of the cataract
cleanses the exhausted body and mind,

focus crystallizes. I harden to you; my passion
swept up in re-formation,

shaped and sharpened beyond reason.
This elemental journey

against the brilliance of so much light
casts in sharp silhouette who I am.

My rumbled conviction reaches so far in,
I know, before I am child of my parents

I am heir to the cataclysm
that forms and reforms this naked beauty.

Dick Bakken

Without Walls

(into black of night with no moon)

She's out here alone
going on nothing but star glow
and gut, each foot-strike
a spark of brightness
down this long
skein of road
in the membrane
of combustion. Focus,
that's the ticket. The map
already laid out above and within.

This is the long run. All the
way through. Blind. Out here alone.

Give me my heart. A little spot
on the earth, a bit of dirt
to meet each stride coming down.
A thousand spats. A vast night
of sparks, dear Lord,
swallowing this black snake of road.
Each inner roseburst an
incandescence
to flash every bite of breath
and rice I've gulped
into this flesh,
out and up from swirled
genesis fathoms with
your wind kissing past me like time
enough, all those violet eyes
my witness.

Aching down dawn's purply rise, she spots
a campfire away across that yon hillside,

then another, another, and another . . .
as gasping she passes the crumpled
promise to all these hands, wet
warrior singlet heaving,
and just pitches over

breathless across
her patch of
our earth.

Annette Velasquez

No Borders...

It was the verdant lushness
that startled my senses-
more than the trepidation
of,
where were we to live?
where to work?
what to eat?

Exiles become accustomed
 to those things...

But, after the desert's
barrenness
the lone cliffs,
endless dust..

Trees hued violet,
crimson hibiscus
oranges ripe in April
rainbow plumed birds,
the colibri, the yellow-breasted, long-legged one,
there, in the marshes
alongside the Rio
all of them welcomed me
to Piedras Negras
nature did,
when no one, no human would.
and this tropical leafiness
snakes even,
undulating gracefully
in muddy water,
floating terrapins
flittering, chittering finches
these things that know
no borders...
enthrall me
in the midst of,
despite of,
hunger and politics
(and those snakes that bear themselves on two legs.)

Janet Ruth

As If They Were Not There

We fly, easily, south across political borders to Veracruz and Oaxaca, Mexico, to partake of a visual and auditory feast, an ornithological orgy of feathered messengers who defy boundaries, both physical and political. We marvel at the beauty and diversity of birds—large and small, resplendently plumaged and subtly brown, familiar and strange. Some live their entire lives south of "our" borders—great curassow, bare-throated tiger-heron, azure-crowned hummingbird, scarlet macaw, green shrike-vireo, crimson-collared tanager. For two-thirds of the year they live side-by-side with migratory birds. Both consume food from the same neotropical menu—nectar, insects fleeing ant swarms, exotic fruits, fish, and seeds; they share habitats that produce these bountiful banquets—from sere tropical deciduous forest to dripping rainforest and mangrove swamp, grassland to montane coniferous forest. Then, leaving wintering grounds, swallow-tailed kite, ruby-throated hummingbird, barn swallow, hermit thrush, orange-crowned warbler, and summer tanager wing across mountains, plains, seas, and walls, biannual immigrants, to gorge on summer plenty and breed in the U.S. and Canada—these birds we call "ours" for one-third of the year. On the wheel of life, in the circle of seasons, walls are meaningless. Ancient biological demands of avian migration roll over physical obstacles as if they were not there.

We live in a country of people from many places, many cultures—some have been here since before written history, some migrated here with dreams, others were dragged here in nightmares. All faced cultural, physical, and political obstacles. Where we succeed in welcoming, sharing, and understanding our differences—taste of kimchi and curry, music of oud and kalimba, spectacle of corn dance and Japanese Noh, love of whatever god we worship—diversity tantalizes our senses, arouses our imaginations, and ravishes our hearts.

Walls of steaming rice divide
the platter, separate three thick pools,
chunks of chicken swim
in Oaxacan *mole,* a spread for the senses,
a feast reminiscent of feathery hues—
    almendrado, creamy blonde head
        of chestnut-colored woodpecker,
    coloradito, rich red deeper than hepatic tanager wings,
    negro, the bittersweet chocolate-brown of Sumichrast's wren.
Rice walls stand, built kernel by kernel
in a kitchen roiling with spicy aromas and savory broths—
    to make a visual impression,
    separate color and flavor,
    facilitate taste comparison.

But barricades must fall.
Tearing down, consuming walls
saturated in almonds, chiles, or chocolate
is part of the gustatory experience.
Unavoidable mélange
    sweet and sharp, dark and bright,
        dips and flutters in my nose like swallows,
yellow with red, and red with black
    swirl and marble, eddy and merge
        in rivulets on my tongue,
    like rivers of migrating raptors above
the Isthmus of Tehuantepec—

a miracle.

Kate Marco

leap

for those of us
who have no voice,
I'll walk these streets
and shout your names,

for those of us
behind the wall,
I will dig and dig
the tunnel long,

for those of us
lost in the dark,
I will hang the sun
along our path,

for those of us
about to jump,
I will be the net
to break your fall,

for those of us
without a home,
I will build a space
to lay your heads,

for all of us
about to bleed,
I will be a mother
to your wounds,

these acts
are not heroic
or beyond
our human realm,
they come from
conscious spirits
leaping
toward the light

Andrew Prokop

Clearly Certainly Yes

Does the cool night air shimmer
does a darkened room bring peace

Does the mind wander
far and away
before near
and ever nearer

Does a fire burn deep within
radiating warmth and transformation

Does determination crumble walls
and tear down fences
does a bridge rise up in their place

Clearly
certainly
yes

Bios

(Page numbers in parentheses)

Steve Ausherman (7, 59) is a poet, painter and photographer who resides in New Mexico. He has been thrice nominated for the Pushcart Prize in poetry and has had two chapbooks of his poetry published entitled Creek Bed Blue and Marking the Bend (both published by Encircle Publications).

Dick Bakken (131), born 1941, grew up in MT-WA-OR, but now since 1980 lives a mile high in Bisbee, AZ. Jump hard from his front porch and you'll land in Sonora, Mexico. *The Whiskey Epiphanies: Selected Poems 1963-2013* (www.pleasureboatstudio.com). *Pudding House #226 Greatest Hits 1967-2002* is now available only from dickbakken@yahoo.com.

Megan Baldrige (45) is a retired English teacher, gardener, Japanophile, museum-docenting, garden-loving mom of four grown children, who has lived in Connecticut half her life, and Cedar Crest and Albuquerque the better half of her life.

Margaret M. Baumler (105) is a longstanding member of Just Poets of Rochester, NY, and has been published in *Le Mot Juste* and elsewhere.

The inaugural poet laureate of Albuquerque, **Hakim Bellamy** (3) is also a W. K. Kellogg Foundation Fellow and a Kennedy Center Citizen Artist Fellow. A National Poetry Slam Champion, Bellamy's first collection of poems, *Swear*, was awarded the Tillie Olsen Award for Creative Writing from the Working-Class Studies Association. www.beyondpoetryink.com

Joanne Bodin, Ph.D. (25), is an award-winning author and poet. Her novel *Orchid of the Night* won the 2017 NYC Big Book Award and the New Mexico/Arizona Book Award in LGBT fiction. Her book of poetry, *Piggybacked*, was a finalist in the NM/AZ Book Awards. Her novel *Walking Fish* won the NM Book Award and the International Book Award in LGBT fiction. She is past Vice President of the NM State Poetry Society.

Rich Boucher's poems (39) have appeared in *Gargoyle, The Nervous Breakdown, Apeiron Review, Mas Tequila Review, In Between Hangovers, Menacing Hedge, Cultural Weekly,* and *Tinderbox Poetry Journal,* among others. From the summer of 2016 to the spring of 2017, he served as the Associate Editor and Weekly Poem Curator at *Elbow Room Magazine*.

Karin Bradberry (71, 95) is a retired high school English and Spanish teacher who loves the challenge of expressing herself through poetry forms. She won the 5th Annual Writer's Digest Poetry Award for her villanelle, "Wolves." Karin taught overseas for many years before settling in New Mexico, her favorite state.

Shelly Bryant (19) divides her year between Shanghai and Singapore. Her work includes nine volumes of poetry, two travel guides, one nonfiction work, and one short story collection. She has translated numerous works from Chinese to English, and her translations have been long-listed for the Man Asian Literary Prize (2012) and shortlisted for the Singapore Literature Prize (2016). shellybryant.com

Tina Carlson (79) is a poet and a psychiatric nurse practitioner who lives in Santa Fe. Her book *Ground, Wind, This Body* was published by the University of New Mexico Press in 2017.

Steve Coffman (5) lives on a dirt road in upstate New York. Among his works are his memoir *How to Walk a Pig* (aka *Chicken Justice); Founders v. Bush;* poetry & prose collections: *Peace Meal; Messy Freedom; Off To A Bang; and The Window;* and he's had numerous produced plays.

Deborah Coy (26) has published three books and has been published in several anthologies and online poetry publications. She was an editor for the anthology, *La Llorona*, published by Beatlick Press, which won the New Mexico/Arizona Book Awards for Anthology in 2013.

Michael Czarnecki (2) is a poet, photographer and small press publisher. FootHills Publishing, founded by him in 1986, has released over 400 chapbooks and books of poetry. Michael has made his living solely through the creative word for over two decades. He often journeys from his home in the upper Susquehanna River watershed on poetic tours across America.

Craig Czury (18, 66) lives in N.E. PA and is the author of *Thumb Notes Almanac: Hitchhiking the Marcellus Shale*. His new book, *Fifteen Stones*, is a collection of prose poems from Italy, Chile, and spaces between. More info at craigczury.com

During the day, **Steven Deridder** (94) tutors reading and writing at Sylvan. At night, he is a poet with a passion for photography, currently on vacation from both to finish his first sci-fi novel. His work has most recently been published in Enzigam, Pencil Marks, and *Mo'Joe, Volume 2*.

Mary Dudley (118) received a master's degree in English from SUNY/Stony Brook before moving to Albuquerque, New Mexico, where she earned a Ph.D. in child development across cultures. She has worked with young children and their families for many years. Her poetry has appeared in numerous publications.

Janet Eigner's (129, 130) *What Lasts is the Breath* (2013) was a winner in the AZ-NM Book Awards 2013 and a finalist in the NM Newspaper Women Contest, 2015. She was a Poetry Foundation Poet, was on *American Life in Poetry*, and has published dance articles and reviews. Forthcoming, a collection documenting 12 backpack trips over four decades into Grand Canyon.

Joshua Gage (49) is an ornery curmudgeon from Cleveland. His first full-length collection, *breaths*, is available from VanZeno Press. *Intrinsic Night* from Sam's Dot Publishing; *Inhuman: Haiku from the Zombie Apocalypse* from Poet's Haven Press; *Necromancy* from Moria Press. He has an MFA in Creative Writing from Naropa University, a penchant for Pendleton shirts and any poem strong enough to yank the breath out of his lungs.

Teresa E. Gallion (30) has been published in numerous journals and anthologies. She has two CDs, *On the Wings of the Wind* and *Poems from Chasing Light*, and three books: *Walking Sacred Ground, Contemplation in the High Desert and Chasing Light*. The latter was a finalist in the 2013 NM/AZ Book Awards. You may preview her work at: http://bit.ly/1aIVPNq or http://bit.ly/13IMLGh

Renny Golden (123) is a writer, professor emerita, poet, and social justice activist. Her books reflect concerns for those made voiceless or marginalized. "I grew up in Chicago on the Southeast side influenced by an Irish grandfather who co-founded Local 399 (originally the 'Micks' who shoveled coal into furnaces) and an Irish grandmother who was a *seanchai* (story-teller)."

Vincent F. A. Golphin (27), who teaches and writes in Central Florida, is included in *Trumped* and *Hers*, earlier volumes in this series. He is also in *Mo' Joe: The Joe the Poet Anthology* (Beatlick Press, 2014). FootHills Publishing released *Ten Stories Down* (2012), poems based on his stays in Beijing, and *Like A Dry Land: A Soul's Journey through the Middle East* (2005), inspired by a visit to Jordan.

Larry Goodell (42) is a poet of performance and page, raconteur of earth's debacle from human greed, satirist of government secrecy and local real estate development, pianist, song-writer, playwright, performance poetry organizer, native of Roswell (1935) and resident of Placitas since 1963, a life-long organic gardener and founder of duende press. See www.larrygoodell.com/ and www.granarybooks.com/collections/goodell/

Kenneth P. Gurney (48) lives in Albuquerque, NM, USA with his beloved Dianne. His latest collection of poems is *Stump Speech* (2015).

Mina Hatami (98) is an Iranian American writer whose poems tell a story of tension along the continuum of doubt certitude love and hate. She is active with the Just Poets organization in Rochester, NY.

Ceinwen E. Cariad Haydon (11) writes poems and short stories (11) She has been published in print anthologies and online. She graduated with an MA in Creative Writing from Newcastle University, UK, in Dec. 2017.

M.J. Iuppa (91) directs the Visual-and-Performing-Arts Minor Program and is a Lecturer in Creative Writing at St. John Fisher College and also teaches Creative Writing at SUNY/Brockport. She has five chapbooks and three full-length poetry collections: *Small Worlds Floating* (2016) and *Within Reach* (2010) both from Cherry Grove Collections; *Night Traveler*, FootHills Publishing, 2003. She lives on a small farm in Hamlin NY.

Mary Strong Jackson's (84, 128) work has appeared in journals and anthologies in the US and England. Her chapbooks include *From Other Tongues, The Never-Ending Poem, Witnesses, No Buried Dogs, Between Door and Frame*, and *Clippings*. Read more at strongjacksonpoet.wordpress.com. Mary lives near Santa Fe, NM.

Kitty Jospé (15) completed her MFA in poetry at Pacific University in 2009 and has published 4 books. Her poems appear in *Nimrod, Grasslimbs, Vehicle, Poetrybay, Centrifugal Eye,* and multiple anthologies. For her, poetry is an effective art for channeling words to carry meanings that strike at the heart.

Faith Kaltenbach (37) attended Bennington College and the Arboretum School of the Barnes Foundation. She is semi-retired and recently began writing seriously. Her work appears in the anthology *Weaving the Terrain: 100-Word Southwestern Poetry*. She enjoys her poetry community, nature, grandchildren and silence.

Kathamann (20) is a returned Peace Corps Volunteer/Afghanistan and a retired registered nurse. She has been active in the Santa Fe arts community for 30 years, exhibiting in juried, group and solo exhibits (kathamann.com). Her poems have occasionally been published in local and regional anthologies.

Herb Kauderer (34) is an associate professor of English at Hilbert College and lives near the US border of Canada. In fact, he is married to a Canadian, proving that borders are not nearly so dividing as some would have us believe.

Mary Elizabeth Lang (116) is a retired college instructor living in Connecticut. She earned her MFA from Bennington College Writing Seminars. Her poems have appeared in many journals, including *Ekphrasis, The Prose Poem*, and *Comstock Review*. Her first book of poetry, *Under Red Cedars*, was published by Little Red Tree Publishing. Her second book, *Permanent Guests*, is coming out this spring.

Gayle Lauradunn's (28) *Reaching for Air* was named a Finalist for Best First Book of Poetry by the Texas Institute of Letters. Her second collection, *All the Wild and Holy: a Life of Eunice Williams, 1696-1785* (FootHills Publishing), received Honorable Mention for the May Sarton Poetry Prize. A chapbook, *Duncan Canal, Alaska*, was published by Grandma Moses Press.

Wayne Lee (68) lives Hillsboro, Oregon. Lee's poems have appeared in *Pontoon, Tupelo Press, Adobe Walls* and other publications. He won the 2012 Fischer Poetry Prize and his collection *The Underside of Light* was a finalist for the 2014 New Mexico/Arizona Book Award in Poetry. More info at wayneleepoet.com

Lyn Lifshin (72, 73) has published over 130 books and chapbooks including 3 from Black Press: *Cold Comfort, Before it's Light*, and *Another Woman who Looks Like Me*. Recent books include *Refugee: The Land and Home That Was Taken Away, Secretariat; Knife Edge & Absinthe; Malala; A Girl Goes into the Woods; Femme Eternal;* and *Little Dancer: the Degas Poems*. She edited 3 anthologies: *Tangled vines, Lips Unsealed; Ariadne's Thread*.
Her web: www: lynlifshin.com

Jane Lipman's (102) first full-length book, *On the Back Porch of the Moon*, Black Swan Editions, won the 2013 NM/AZ Book Award and a NM Press Women's Award. Her chapbooks, *The Rapture of Tulips* and *White Crow's Secret Life*, were finalists for NM Book Awards in 2009 and 2010. She founded and directed Taos Institute, sponsoring workshops by Robert Bly, Joseph Campbell, Gioia Timpanelli, Paul Winter, and others.

Douglas Lipton (67) was born and educated in Glasgow. He has spent most of his working life in Dumfriesshire as an English Teacher, Special Educational Needs Teacher and FE college Educational Support Worker. He began writing poetry in his teens, and attended the famed Glasgow University Adult Education creative writing class inaugurated by Philip Hobsbaum.

Ellaraine Lockie's (10) *Where the Meadowlark Sings* won the 2014 Encircle Publications chapbook contest. She also received the Women's National Book Association's Poetry Prize and San Gabriel Poetry Festival award, among others. Her thirteenth chapbook, *Tripping with the Top Down*, was recently released by Foothills Publishing. Ellaraine teaches poetry workshops and serves as Poetry Editor for the magazine *Lilipoh*.

John Macker (75, 77) is the author of seven full-length books of poetry including, most recently *Blood in the Mix* (with El Paso poet Lawrence Welsh). He was also a contributing editor to *Malpais Review*. He has contributed poems to Denver woodblock artist Leon Loughridge's 2017 eight-volume woodblock folio series, *Gorge Songs*.

Dennis Maloney (110, 111) is a poet, translator, and editor/publisher of the widely respected White Pine Press in Buffalo, NY. His poetry volumes include *The Map Is Not the Territory: Poems & Translations, Just Enough, Listening to Tao Yuan Ming* and *Empty Cup*. A new collection, *The Things I Notice Now*, will appear from MadHat Press in 2018. Works of translation include *Neruda's Stones of Chile* and *Between the Floating Mist: Poems of Ryokan*.

Jennifer Maloney (56) started writing poetry, songs and stories when she was a child. She is also a singer (performing with her husband and with an as-yet-unnamed band), and learning to dance burlesque!

Kate Marco (136) has been writing poetry and prose since she learned to put pen to paper. In 1976, Seven Stars published a small book of her poems, *Through The Changes, Gently* (under the name Kathleen Keller), which reached #4 on the small press bestseller list. Kate has published in newspapers and poetry journals for several decades. She was poetry editor for *Artlines* magazine in Taos, New Mexico.

Lori Nolasco Martinez (60, 74) is Italian American by birth, French through her higher education at the Sorbonne, and Dominican thanks to her husband, with whom she travels back to the island. The only walls she sees are those of the gardens in her hometown of Rochester, New York. She is the author of two books from FootHills Publishing, *Ariadne of the Freezing Rains* and *Demetrio's Scythe*.

Mary McGinnis (9) has been writing and living in New Mexico since 1972. Having the disability of blindness all her life challenged her to have a career. Besides appearing in over 70 magazines and anthologies, she has published three full-length collections: *Listening for Cactus* (1996), *October Again* (2008), and *See with Your Whole Body* (2016). She was the first recipient of the Gratitude Award from the NM Literary Arts Board in 2009.

Karla Linn Merrifield (126), a National Park Artist-in-Residence, has 12 books to her credit; the newest is *Bunchberries, More Poems of Canada*. She is assistant editor and book reviewer for *The Centrifugal Eye*. Give her name a Google to read more and visit her at http://karlalinn.blogspot.com

Bill Nevins' poems (12, 124) have appeared in many anthologies and magazines. He has read at venues like the Maple Leaf (New Orleans), Bowery Poetry Café (NYC), and Taos Poetry Circus. His collection *Heartbreak Ridge* was published in 2014 by Swimming with Elephants. He is featured in the 2007 documentary *Committing Poetry in Times of War*. He lives in Albuquerque and also hosts First Tuesday "Fire Angel Sunset Readings" in Angel Fire, NM.

Loren Niemi (97, 112) is an innovative storyteller, author of a poetry chapbook, *Coyote Flies Coach* (Sister Black Press) and *The New Book of Plots* (on the uses of narrative in storytelling and fiction), and co-author with Elizabeth Ellis of the critically acclaimed, *Inviting the Wolf In: Thinking About Difficult Stories*.

Bruce Noll (121, 122) is perhaps best known for his program PURE GRASS, an experience with Whitman's Leaves, which has been seen around the U.S. and other countries for the past 48 years. His own poetry has appeared in numerous journals and anthologies; his newest books include *Circumference of Light*, *Notes to My Mortician*, and *The American Entomologists Poets' Guide to the Orders of Insects*. He lives in Albuquerque.

Maril Nowak (92) lives in the middle of New York State, the middle of nowhere, trying to imagine the middle, left, and right of Somewhere Else who voted for The Bloviator. She takes great comfort in Mencken's words. Americans survived Warren Harding, the original bloviator; we will survive this one too.

Jules Nyquist (1, 53, 85) is the founder of Jules' Poetry Playhouse, a place for poetry and play in Albuquerque where Jules teaches poetry classes and hosts visiting writers. She took her MFA from Bennington College. Jules' poems have appeared in *5 AM, Salamander, Malpais Review, Adobe Walls, A View from the Loft, Gray Sparrow, House Organ, Duke City Fix, Café Review* and others. Her website is www.julesnyquist.com

Stuart A. Paterson (86) is a widely anthologised Scottish poet living on the Galloway coast. He was BBC Scotland's Poet-in-Residence 2017-2018. His first Scots language collection, *Aye*, was published by Tapsalteerie in 2016. *Looking South*, poems about Galloway, was published by Indigo Dreams Publishing in 2017, and *Heelster-gowdie/beul-fo-bhonn*, poems in Scots and Gaelic (with Marcas Mac an Tuarneir) by Tapsalteerie in 2017. For 30 years he's been writing about & actively supporting the campaign for Scottish independence. https://en-gb.facebook.com/patersonpoetry/

Don Paul (113) is the author of more than 25 books and the leader or producer of 23 albums. Many are available through New Orleans' Louisiana Music Factory. His most recent musical collaborations are with the GALLOP Trio and the Rivers of Dreams band. His website is donpaulwearerev.com

Colleen Powderly's (89) early poems reflecting her childhood in the Deep South and years spent in the Midwest form the basis for her book *Split*, published by FootHills Publishing (2009). Recent work focuses on stories from the working class, particularly from women's lives. She lives in Rochester NY.

Andrew Prokop (137) is a communications engineer and software developer by day and a writer of poetry and prose in the wee hours of the morning. He was born in the Arizona desert, but has called Minnesota home for the past 30 years. Clearly, he is a man of great extremes.

William Pruitt (31) has been publishing poems for 40 years in such places as *Ploughshares, Country Journal, Longhouse*, and *Stoneboat Journal*, and fiction more recently in journals such *Midway, Hypertext, Visitant*. He is also a storyteller who has written & performed original stories about Frederick Douglass, Susan B. Anthony, Mary Jemison and Daniel Boone.

Randy Prus (17, 120) says: "American politics died with John Quincy Adams, the greatest and least productive president in our history, ushering in American nationalism and its empire. I write in its shadow." He teaches English at Southeastern Oklahoma State University.

Sylvia Ramos Cruz (62) is a Puerto Rican mother, grandmother, surgeon, women's rights activist, gardener, world traveler, friend and lover. Her poems, eclectic in form and content, are inspired by works of art in all its forms, women's lives, and every-day injustices. She loves words and what they can do.

Margaret Randall (23, 108): Her most recent book of poems is *The Morning After: Poetry & Prose in a Post-Truth World* (Wings Press 2017). Duke University Press published her bilingual anthology of eight decades of Cuban poetry, *Only the Road/Solo el camino* (2016) and *Exporting Revolution: Cuba's Global Solidarity* (2017). In 2018 Wings will bring out her *Selected Poems*, celebrating 60 years of poetry published in 30 collections, which she will launch in September at City Lights Books in San Francisco.

John Roche (33, 78, 107) is the author of *On Conesus, Topicalities, Road Ghosts, and The Joe Poems: The Continuing Saga of Joe the Poet*, as well as the author of *Mo' Joe: The Anthology*. He believes we are going to need poetry to get through the next four years or forty years.

Janet Ruth (38, 100, 134) is an emeritus research ornithologist from Corrales, NM. She has published scientific papers on bird ecology and natural history essays. Her writing focuses on connections to the natural world. Recent poems were published in *Grey Sparrow Journal, Value: Essays, Stories & Poems by Women of a Certain Age*, and *Santa Fe Literary Review*. She also had poems published in two previous volumes of the Poets Speak anthologies—*Hers* and *Water*.

Georgia Santa Maria (50) is a Native New Mexican, and has been an artist and writer most of her life. In 2012 she was a Guest Editor for LUMMOX Poetry Anthology, Issue I. Her book of poetry and photographs, *Lichen Kisses*, was published in 2013, and her book *Dowsing* is just out. Recently, she was first runner-up for the LUMMOX 5 Poetry Prize.

Celeste Helene Schantz (61) has work which appears in *Stone Canoe, One Throne Magazine*, and is upcoming in the WAVES anthology from AROHO. She has studied with Marge Piercy and Kim Addonizio. She lives in Upstate New York and is currently working on her first book of poetry.

Marc Schillace's (4) love of learning has taken him from the study of art and eastern philosophy at Rhode Island School of Design to Oxford University where he read Shakespeare and philosophical anthropology. He finds writing poetry to be the most satisfying way to express his feelings and develop his ideas about experience and the meaning of existence.

Gretchen Schulz (58) is an Activist Artist at Large.

G.E. Schwartz (109), noted performance artist and author of *Only Others Are: Poems* (Legible Press), *World* (Furniture Press), *Odd Fish* (Argotist Editions), and *Thinking in Tongues* (Hank's Loose Gravel Press), was born in Pottsville, Pennsylvania, 1958.

Patricia Roth Schwartz (90) lives in the Finger Lakes. Her seven books of poems include *Charleston Girls, a Memoir in Poems of a West Virginia Childhood*, and *The Crows of Copper John, a History of Auburn Prison in Poems*, and a 2017 chapbook, *Know Better: poems of resistance*. From 2001 to 2015, she facilitated an inmates' poetry workshop inside Auburn Correctional Facility. She is currently writing a memoir, *Soul Knows No Bars*, about this experience.

Katherine DiBella Seluja's (21) work has appeared in *bosque, Broadsided Press, Crab Creek Review* and *Santa Fe Literary Review*, among others. Her poem, "Letter to my suegra from Artesia, New Mexico" won honorable mention in the *Santa Ana River Review* contest, judged by Juan Felipe Herrera. Her first collection, *Gather the Night*, is forthcoming from UNM Press in 2018.

Eugene Stelzig (8) is Distinguished Teaching Professor of English Emeritus at SUNY Geneseo. His poetry has appeared during the past six decades in a variety of little and literary magazines. He has also published two collections: *Fool's Gold: Selected Poems of a Decade* (FootHills, 2008), and *Assorted Selfscriptings 1964-1985* (Milne Library, SUNY Geneseo, 2015).

Eleanor Grogg Stewart (54, 119) was a classical actress with an MA in theater. When she came to NM in 1970, her trickle of poems became a flood. She taught English comp at UNM and also published a book, *Not Only a Refugee*, about teaching English at a Vietnamese refugee camp in the Philippines. She published a book of poems, *Falling into Enchantment*, in 2014, and a second book of poems called *She Tells Us Stories* in 2017.

Nathanael William Stolte (93) is the author of *A Beggar's Book of Poems, Bumblebee Petting Zoo, Fools' Song, Origami Creature, & A Beggar's Prayer Book*. His poems have appeared in *Ghost City Review, Guide to Kulture, Trailer Park Quarterly*, and *In Between Hangovers*, among others. He is Acquisitions Editor for CWP Collective Press. Stolte was voted best poet in Buffalo by *Artvoice* in 2016. He is a madcap, flower-punk, D.I.Y. Buffalo-bred & corn-fed poet.

Robbie Sugg (55) grew up in the San Francisco Bay Area. His poetry has appeared in journals including *Elohi Gadugi, Earthen Lamp* (India), *The Café Review, Cape Cod Poetry Review, The Newport Review*, and *Flying Fish*. His first book, *Koccha and Other Poems*, was published in 2014 by DaysEye Press. His artwork has been exhibited throughout the US and England. He currently resides in Albuquerque.

Martha Treichler (6) is a retired teacher and a retired Registered Dietitian. She lives on a farm on a hill near Hammondsport, NY. During the 1948-49 school year, she studied with Charles Olson at Black Mountain College. Martha has published five books of poems with FootHills Publishing.

Roslye Ultan (36) draws on her visual background, and interest in nature to write poetry on the wonders of everyday life. She fills a white page with color, form, and the rhythm of existence. Ultan is Senior Faculty at the University of Minnesota in Art History and Visual Culture; curator of exhibitions on the intersection of art and the environment.

Annette Velasquez (133) was born in Urbana, Illinois, the daughter of Hungarian refugees. She served a brief stint in the United States Marine Corps and was honorably discharged. Her forthcoming trilogy *Daughter of Diasporas* is due out shortly. She is a member of Tumblewords Writer's workshop and lives in El Paso.

R. B. Warren (13) has been published in *The Rag, Duke City Fix*, the 2011 *Fixed and Free Anthology, Overthrowing Capitalism: Vol.2*, and has a full-length collection, *Litanies Not Adopted*, published by Swimming with Elephants Publications.

Stewart S. Warren (114), author of over 20 poetry collections, is a drifter and evocateur whose work is both personal and transpersonal with a mystic undercurrent. Stewart is the owner of Mercury HeartLink, an independent New Mexico press for discriminating writers that supports them in realizing their artistic visions.

Denise Weaver Ross (cover) is an artist, poet and graphic designer who lives and works in Albuquerque. Her images are richly layered with cultural, political, and historical references. Denise graduated from UMass–Amherst with an MFA, regularly exhibits in the Southwest, and contributes her design abilities to local writers, artists and galleries. Her art and poetry can also be found in many in local and international magazines and anthologies.

Lawrence Welsh (76) has published nine books of poetry, including *Begging for Vultures: New and Selected Poems, 1994-2009* (UNM Press). This collection won the New Mexico-Arizona Book Award. It was also named a Notable Book by Southwest Books of the Year and a finalist for both the PEN Southwest Book Award and Writers' League of Texas Book Award.

Cullen Whisenhunt (43) is an adjunct instructor of remedial English at Southeastern Oklahoma State University.

Bart White (82) teaches Spanish and French, and is President of Just Poets in Rochester, NY. Married to an immigrant, father of two children (one adopted from China), he is grateful to be both an American and a citizen of the world. He is co-editor of *Birdsong: Poems in celebration of birds* and author of *The Faces We Had as Children* (both from FootHills Publishing)

Scott Wiggerman (81) is author of three books of poetry, *Leaf and Beak: Sonnets; Presence;* and *Vegetables and Other Relationships*; and editor of *Wingbeats: Exercises & Practice in Poetry; Lifting the Sky;* and *Bearing the Mask*. Recent poems appeared in *Naugatuck River Review, Red Earth Review, bosque, shuf,* and *Yellow Chair Review*. He is an editor for Dos Gatos Press of Albuquerque.

Dwain Wilder's (115) publications include *Under the Only Moon* and poems in *Kudzu Review, Shadow/Play, Le Mot Juste, Lake Affect, Hot Air and Zen Bow*. He is past editor of *Zen Bow*, and co-edited *Liberty's Vigil: The Occupy Anthology*, and Vig*il for the Marcellus Shale*. Dwain lives in a small cottage beside a large dark forest.

Pamela Williams (88) is a poet and visual artist, with a lifelong habit of artistic expression. After thirty expansive years in the San Francisco area, New Mexico's extreme contrasts and rich history are providing alchemical inspiration and empowerment, fueling her poetry/assemblages, her Etsy shop, NextSegue, and her first collection of poetry, *Hair on Fire*, available at Amazon.com.

Linda Yen (103) is a retired poverty lawyer who writes poetry on the sly. She somehow managed to publish in a few small presses and has received several awards for her poems.

Neil Young (24, 64) hails from Belfast and now lives in northeast Scotland, where he is co-founder of *The Poets' Republic* magazine. His first collection, *Lagan Voices*, was published in 2011 (Scryfa), followed by *The Parting Glass - Fourteen Sonnets* (Tapsalteerie) in 2016. A new slim volume, *Jimmy Cagney's Long-Lost Kid Half-Brother*, appeared in 2017 (Black Light Engine Room).

Leah Zazulyer (69, 96) writes poetry, prose, translates Yiddish poetry, and was a special education teacher and school psychologist. She lives in Rochester, NY, but grew up in California in a bilingual family from Belarus. She has published 5 poetry books and 2 books of translations of Israel Emiot.

Professor **Kevin Zepper** (87) teaches at Minnesota State University Moorhead. He has authored four chapbooks of poetry and is a part of the music/poetry duo Lines&Notes. Some of his recent photo credits include: *Red Weather, Inscape* and *Portage Magazine*.

JULES' POETRY PLAYHOUSE PUBLICATIONS
Jules Nyquist is the founder and operator of Jules' Poetry Playhouse in Albuquerque, NM, a place for poetry and play
http://www.julesnyquist.com

&

BEATLICK PRESS

Writers with Something to Say
Beatlick Press was established in 2011 to honor the memory of Beatlick Joe Speer of Albuquerque, New Mexico and continue his artistic mission to publish deserving writers:

Pamela Adams Hirst, publisher
Beatlick Press
Albuquerque, NM
http://beatlick.com/

Made in the USA
San Bernardino, CA
12 March 2018